Dream Your Reality is a delightful resource full
of exercises and techniques for anyone looking to expand
the power of their dreams.

Jaymi Elford,
author of *Tarot Inspired Life*

• • •

Dream Your Reality from the multitalented Gita Rash
is a fascinating and enlightening exploration. Rash has com-
piled a comprehensive manual complete with action steps to
help each person harness the power of their dreams.

Christiana Gaudet,
author of *Fortune Stellar* and *Tarot Tour Guide*

• • •

Through pop-cultural associations, historical reference,
personal experience, and stories, Gita Rash presents the concept of applying an increased self-awareness to the power of
understanding our dreams and bringing a new reality into
existence. Gita utilizes her knowledge of Vedic astrology, yoga,
palmistry, and psychic practice to provide interesting
and grounded guidance to any seeker embarking on a dream
manifestation journey.

Amber Highland,
publisher of the *Cartomancer Magazine*

GITA RASH

DREAM YOUR
REALITY

Utilize the Subconscious Mind
to Manifest Your Reality

REDFeather™

MIND | BODY | SPIRIT

Cover art: Shutterstock artist Olga Tashlikovich
Type set in Minion
ISBN: 978-0-7643-6699-4

Printed in China

Published by REDFeather Mind, Body, Spirit
An imprint of Schiffer Publishing, Ltd.
4880 Lower Valley Road, Atglen, PA 19310
Phone: (610) 593-1777; Fax: (610) 593-2002
Email: info@redfeathermbs.com
Web: www.redfeathermbs.com

For our complete selection of fine books on this and related subjects, please visit our website at www.redfeathermbs.com. You may also write for a free catalog.

REDFeather Mind, Body, Spirit's titles are available at special discounts for bulk purchases for sales promotions or premiums. Special editions, including personalized covers, corporate imprints, and excerpts, can be created in large quantities for special needs. For more information, contact the publisher.

To my little boy David, who continues to help me
from the other side, and to Schiffer Publishing and REDFeather
for making my dream a reality.

Build a dream and the dream will build you.
—Robert A. Schuller

*There are some people who live in a dream world,
and there are some who face reality; and then there
are those who turn one into the other.*
—Douglas H. Everett

CONTENTS

Foreword

When I was a kid, I was an active dreamer. I dreamt at night. When I dreamt at school, they called me a daydreamer.

When I was a kid, I remembered my dreams every morning. Every morning, as the first pink light cracked over the blinds, I rolled over. With my crusty eyes half closed, I scribbled stray words of a dream to remember, but the dream faded anyway, a piece of nighttime magic that wouldn't speak on the notebook paper.

When I was a kid, the possibilities of dreams, the meanings of them, got stuck in my head. I became lodged between social-psychological explanations and metaphysical ones. I could not see that the two are interwoven through history. I loved the scientism of the psychoanalytic concepts, but I turned to my Encyclopedia of Dreams more often. I enjoyed the mystical understandings of dreams. I liked the clarity of them, the simplicity, the directness, the mystery.

Nowadays, I am a sociologist. Sociology (and other disciplines agree!) declares that humans are social animals. We rely on each other. Our perception of the collective and our place in the collective shape our identities, self-worth, and life outcomes. Important precepts in social psychology and sociology fuse with the insights of this book, and students of these fields, as well as metaphysics, benefit from their intersection and the acknowledgment of their compatible concepts. For example, like the sciences, *Dream Your Reality* uncovers the historical relationship between prophecy and "madness" and encourages us to excavate the subconscious. Like debates of "nature versus nurture," now retired for more holistic perspectives, Rash teaches us that we are all capable of "magical" abilities, even if some "birth positions" make it easier or harder. This is something that is true in both the organization of society and the contours of astrology.

Gita Rash deftly situates all themes and knowledges, across time and space, to instruct readers on how to understand and interpret their dreams. These ways include (but are not limited to) finding talents through dream states or using dreams as portals to connect to the beloved dead, to past lives, or to the future. According to Rash, working closely with dreams can even help one fulfill their political ambitions.

Dream Your Reality also seamlessly marries Eastern and Western perspectives, offering insights on chakras and mudras, crystal healing, astrology, palmistry, Tarot, ESP, psychometry, apparitions, and more. Each seemingly disparate avenue folds back into the emphasis on understanding our subconscious and dream states. *Dream*

Your Reality teaches us how to decode personal dreams for our highest good, adding practical application to the theoretical arguments.

Nowadays, I don't remember my dreams. This book motivates me to do better. It promises our potential to make manifest the desires that lie quiet in the subconscious mind. It offers a compelling argument for why dreams are crucial keys to exploring our health and identity, and how our dreams can help us deepen our understanding of ourselves and others. Best of all, Gita Rash speckles her insights with accounts of her own dream states and experiences with paranormal phenomena. She tells us that the "cosmos" reaches out to us when we are low, and lifts us up with the wisdom of the endless universe.

But not if you don't reach for it.

Reach for it in this book.

Melissa F. Lavin, PhD,
Associate professor of sociology, State University of New York

Acknowledgments

I am grateful to Spirit and the countless voices from beyond for their inspiration and encouragement in authoring this book and to my husband, Dave, for his constant love and support.

Introduction

Einstein said, "For many years my fellow scientists were annoyed by my contention that imagination—that which occurs within our minds—was more important than knowledge."

In the book *Beyond Biofeedback*, the author says, "The unconscious mind did not distinguish between an imagined and a real experience" (Green 1989).

In psychoanalytic terms, the unconscious includes only things that are repressed from conscious thought. On the other hand, the subconscious includes all the information that cannot be fully, consciously processed, and can include behavioral patterns and habits, just as it is believed that hypnosis can be used to work on these habits and change them and their behavior in the future. There has been an ongoing debate between the technical meaning of unconscious and subconscious. A discussion of the fine line between unconscious and subconscious is not the purpose of this book. I will leave it to the scientists and psychoanalysts. Since they have already been used interchangeably, that would be my approach from the perspective of a psychic medium. My belief is that the subconscious mind contains information that is like a submarine, under the surface of the mind. Information that you may know but are unaware of. Important and helpful information that you can find like a missing key.

This substantiates the power of the subconscious mind, which is a powerful warehouse of everything we experience and feel. Our daily interactions, encounters, and adventures feed our subconscious constantly, updating it and filling in the blanks as needed. Meditation and hypnosis are two common, well-known ways of accessing the subconscious mind and drawing upon this information. The third key to the subconscious mind is dreaming. Dreams are like a vast, deep, never-ending ocean full of all kinds of treasures. A treasure chest that you can open at will, tapping into your own resources to find the tools you need to achieve your dreams! Whether you desire to have love, abundance, a successful career, a fulfilling relationship, that dream home, or good health or spiritual guidance or to overcome addictions, such as smoking, drinking, even eating chocolate, you can dream it and achieve it!

Parts of us are in the future, and sometimes we literally perceive that future. Also called prescience, future vision or future sight is the ability to see events in the future. As a mysterious and enigmatic subject, it is at the same time mesmerizing and enthralling, giving us a preview of future events, almost like the trailer of a film to be released. Ancient African, Native American, Aboriginal, and several tribal cultures around the world go to great lengths to access a vivid dream state to receive messages and hints of the future. History abounds with cases of many personalities who transformed the world with the inspiration they received in precognitive dreams. Personalities such as Abraham Lincoln, Joan of Arc, and Albert Einstein, to name a few.

Much has been said and written about precognitive dreams and déjà vu. In this experience a place, an event, or a person or people you meet for the first time may seem oddly familiar, like you have been there before or met that person before. You cannot pinpoint this sense of familiarity, this nostalgic feeling that gives you an illusion of precognition, because you think you have already experienced it. Dreams are precognitive if you experience the same thing in the future. They usually have no precursor; they happen randomly. They could be warnings of an event to come, so you might anticipate and react accordingly when it does happen. On the flip side, they are not always warnings of a foreboding nature. They could even be beautiful, enchanting, and fascinating. However colorful and bizarre they may sometimes seem, coincidence they are not. Some of the more well-known precognitive dreams recorded have been of world events, groups of people collectively dreaming of the same event yet to come. One such example is the attack on the Twin Towers on 9/11. This phenomenon has been attributed to the power of the collective consciousness. A shared understanding of certain beliefs and ideals by a group of people created by a sense of solidarity, community, and a connection to each other expressed as a unifying force. Many people have posted accounts claiming to have had precognitive dreams of the September 11 attacks on websites such as Quora.

The subconscious is motivated by emotion, not reason, and by suggestion and feeling. Groups of people can simultaneously have the same dream and can also share a group dream just as an activity is shared in real life. In the 2010 Christopher Nolan film *Inception* the concept of entering a mind through the dream state and influencing it and coercing it has been portrayed, where the lead character, Cobb, played by Leonardo DiCaprio, plans a heist by planting the idea of his scheme through a series of suggestions in the mind of the character named Fischer. This film describes a dream within a dream within a dream as the plot is executed as planned. Dream suggestion and collaboration have been explored in this film. There are several layers and levels of the various concepts and aspects of the human mind and body in the dream state. Some of the actions portrayed in the film are actualities, like feeling the emotions of events physically outside the dream.

I lost my mother as a young adult and, being extremely close to her, was devastated at not having her guidance in my life, which I was about to begin as an adult.

Desperately wanting to communicate with her, I accidentally discovered a means of connecting through dreams. Since I emigrated shortly thereafter, I lived for most of my life away from my dad as well. After he passed, I now have an almost virtual line to both my parents, who are there for me whenever I need them for advice, guidance, and support. This spurred me to dig deeper and explore the mysterious world of dreaming over the years. Dreams and dream interpretation have now become a passion for me, as I advise and teach through webinars and private group sessions. As an avid dreamer, I never cease to be fascinated by the new discoveries and learning that dreams provide. Dreams not only have guided and advised me spiritually on my journey in life but have also provided me with practical material benefits that make life comfortable. My relationships have benefited vastly from the knowledge dreams have provided. Furthermore, dreams have uncovered latent talents in me that probably would have been left unrecognized otherwise.

Another life-changing event I experienced in life was a near-death experience. A week after I buried my newborn son, I suffered a postpartum hemorrhage. On the way to the emergency room, I lost consciousness. During that time, I found myself in a large room filled with people, relatives and friends who had passed on. I could clearly see my mother and the grandmother of a friend who recently died in a terroristic bomb blast. The atmosphere felt so warm, cozy, peaceful, and loving. I hugged as many people as I could and really felt overjoyed at finding this new home. I was all set to settle in and hang my hat, when I noticed some people with stern expressions seated around a table in boardroom fashion. These were not people I recognized. They told me in a kind but firm manner that I should go back. I asked them why and they replied, "Because you have to teach." This was mind boggling to me. At the time, I was working in one of the largest financial companies, I loved my job, and I thought I would retire doing what I loved to do. Besides, there was nothing I knew enough about to teach, not to mention the fact that teaching never crossed my mind. The next thing I knew, I was on a gurney being wheeled into the operating room, as people were yelling my name. It may have been only a few seconds that I lost consciousness, but it seemed much longer than that. The experience was so blissful and profound, it made an indelible impression on my mind.

This event changed my life: I was no longer the hard-core finance professional running around to achieve goals and targets. With the realization that there were so many more dimensions other than this physical plane, I started to seriously study esoteric and metaphysical subjects, broadening my faculties with time. Along with other modalities, I found dreams to be a magnificent medium of accessing amazing information and knowledge that has contributed greatly to my development. Having vivid, detailed dreams as a child, I literally grew up with a sort of double life, one during the day and another at night. Being too young to comprehend the meaning or purpose of dreams, I simply enjoyed them as colorful dramas that I thought of as entertainment. Aging, maturing, and life experiences led me toward understanding the power and deeper meaning of dreams and their profound significance. With the experience of numerous prophetic dreams, yet another dimension of intricacy revealed itself. Dreams have provided me with a link to the other side, to communicate with my loved ones, spirit guides, masters, and teachers, who have guided, supported, and encouraged me on my life path. This has strengthened, inspired, and motivated me to pass on my learning and share it with others.

The Power of Dreams

Life is a dream and dream is reality! Maya, as the Hindus believe, is the sequence of events and circumstances in one's life and environment, when we are constantly dreaming. Madame Blavatsky, the Russina mystic and author, is quoted as saying, "Knowledge *comes in visions, first in dreams, and then in pictures presented to the inner eye through meditation*" (Blavatsky 1910).

According to ancient Sanskrit texts, when we realize that we are constantly dreaming, we open to a greater awareness. This awareness can be utilized in multiple ways for spiritual growth, material abundance, and greater well-being.

If you can create your own reality, why can't you *dream* your own reality? Everything starts with a dream. To quote Martin Luther King Jr., *"I have a dream."* Imagine the power this statement holds. The Ottoman Empire, which became a dominant power in Europe and the Middle East, was one of the largest and most influential empires and survived for more than six centuries, starting in the early twelfth century and is a classic example of how such a magnificent empire could be built on the basis of a dream. Ertugrul, the leader, rose from the status of a mere nomad and shepherd to laying down the foundation of what was to become a formidable Islamic empire. According to the Ottoman chronicles, the son of Ertugul, Osman, who was also envisioned in a dream by Ertugrul himself, had a dream in which a fully formed tree emerged from his body, "*and its shade compassed the world,*" which he envisioned as a vast empire that he could establish and create for his tribe. The tree here is symbolic of the human psyche. Constantinople (modern-day Istanbul), which was the seat of power of Europe, was captured by the descendants of Osman following the dream. In addition to fulfilling his political ambitions, Osman's dreams also materialized romantically, since he married the daughter of a neighboring sheikh who was at first quite reluctant to give his daughter to Osman. This is the stuff dreams are made of. There are many more fascinating instances in the history of the Ottoman Empire, where strategic operations were conceived in the dream state, as well as similar instances in other empires and cultures around the world. The runaway success of the historic drama *Diliris Ertugrul* on Netflix may have also been dreamt by the producer of this international hit. I reference this example since this is a dramatization of a historical theme in our current time.

There are numerous such accounts of inventors, novelists, dramatists, and creators, artists, et al., who have all utilized their dreams and inspirations during sleep to invent and create many wonderful things which we enjoy, utilize, and depend on today. Even the father of psychology and dreaming, Carl Jung, has had profound life-changing dreams that he described in his self-published book *Septum Sermons and Mortuos (The Seven Sermons to the Dead)*. He credits his dreams as the forerunner of all his works. To quote him, "All my works, all my creative activity has come from those initial fantasies and dreams which began in 1912, almost fifty years ago. Everything that I accomplished later in life, was already contained in them, although at first only in the form of emotions and images." (Jung 1916, p. 192).

Another example I would like to illustrate is the heroic account of Harriet Tubman, who had vivid dreams and visions that she successfully translated into a well-devised scheme of developing underground maps and rescuing slaves. To her credit, she led over three hundred slaves to freedom as an Underground Railroad conductor, which was quite revolutionary for the time and earned her the title of "Moses." In addition, she was the only woman to lead an armed expedition in the Civil War. What an admirable feat in an age that was not exactly open to this kind of a courageous display from women.

THE SLEEP PROCESS

We go to bed every night, a daily ritual that we perform just like brushing our teeth when we wake up in the morning. What happens when our minds stop chattering and we eventually fall asleep? As we fall into a light slumber, we are still relatively awake and alert; though relaxed, we can still hear noises or sounds. As the brain begins to slow down, alpha waves are produced. We are in a hypnagogic state where we might sometimes experience those jerks or falling movements. Then we move to the next stage, where the brain produces theta waves. In this stage, the brain slows down further and connects to the deeper intuitive abilities, memories, etc. We then move to the next stage, where the heart rate begins to slow, the temperature drops, and breathing and heart rate become more regular. As we move into the deepest sleep cycle, the muscles relax, blood pressure drops, and breathing slows down. The brain produces delta waves. We become less responsive to noises and other activities around us. Then we enter the REM (rapid eye movement) stage of sleep, where most dream activity occurs, since the body is totally relaxed and immobilized while the brain takes over and becomes more active. The brain starts to defrag the hardware of your body and start the cleanup process. Each night we go through these cycles repeatedly, creating dreams in every REM cycle, which lasts longer as sleep progresses, producing one to six or so dreams per night. In most of the dreams occurring in the REM cycle, as the eyes dart from side to side the brain registers the "drama" of the night, which we refer to as dreams. During the REM cycle the brain is transferring short-term memory to long-term memory, which acts almost like a hard drive of the body.

Everyone dreams, even animals do, but not everyone remembers their dreams. I am often told by people that they do not dream. My reaction is the same when people say they do not have the time to exercise. What they really mean is that they are not interested, or they have other priorities. If you try to pay attention to your dreams, you will remember them. Inculcating a discipline of recording your dreams in a journal, on the computer, or in whatever way is convenient for you will produce far-reaching benefits in your personal life. Technology has made it convenient for us to dictate dreams directly to our cell phones while doing other chores. We lead busy lives and often multitask anyway. Some people dream in black and white, and some in color; if you are one of those dreaming in color, consider it a great gift. Dreams are a gift from the universe. The more you work with them, the better your recall will be. After some practice, you will be able to recall four, five, or even six dreams per night.

External stimuli play a large part in influencing the content of your dreams, while the conscious mind stores all your thoughts, emotions, and experiences during the day and plays it back to you while you sleep at night, almost like a playback system via your subconscious mind. If you engage in some activity just before bedtime, such as watching a television show or chatting on social media and the like, very often that plays out in your dream as well. Which could explain why we often dream of celebrities and people in the news. Sometimes, a change of location could also alter the dream process and regularity. My observation has been that when I go away on vacation, I have fewer dreams. Depending on the environment, the dream seems to dance to the beat of the place. However, for me, there is never a dull moment, whether at home or away. The dream drive never stops. Weakness in the physical body caused by illness, harsh medical treatments, or frequent hospitalizations weakens the aura automatically, which affects the quality and content of dreams. Generally, it is not advisable to undertake lucid or astral voyages when the body is weakened and functioning on a subpar level. I know of experiences where astral visits in a physically weak body have ended up in unforgettable nightmares. This is because the auric egg, known as the etheric body responsible for all out-of-body experiences, is fragmented when the physical body is under stress.

Let's look at some of the benefits of dreaming.

PROBLEM-SOLVING

One of the biggest advantages of dreams is finding a platform for dealing with conflicts, working through them, trying on different solutions, and finding the right answer. Dream characters and archetypes function as costars in your nocturnal production, as you rehearse and hone your scripts to perfection. The opportunity to face the villain (which could sometimes be the self) is presented in the dream context as a means of facing what you may be avoiding in your waking life. As human beings, we like to shelter ourselves by being in denial and avoiding the prospect of acknowledging uncomfortable or negative experiences. All those monsters in your nightmares bring your attention to what is essentially homework for growth and progress. Dealing with negative symbols causing fear and panic in dreams prepares you to deal with dangerous situations in life and provides you with the potential to step out of your comfort zone and attain self-confidence.

HEALTH

Researchers are now acknowledging the health benefits of dreaming. They alleviate depression, uplift and regulate moods, and create an overall sense of joy, bewilderment, and even ecstasy. Dreams are good for a healthy functioning of the brain. The act of remembering, recalling, and recording dreams strengthens memory and cognitive functions. The advantages of REM sleep have been validated in medical and neuroscience journals as therapeutic, allowing patients to be less prone to PTSD, and lowering the risk of developing Alzheimer's disease and dementia. Emotions, even those that are sad in dreams, are real and can be healed while dreaming. This provides an effective way to process the emotions and experiences of the day and release them if there is a need. The numerous health benefits of dreaming and REM sleep have been researched and analyzed by many labs and institutions, describing the advantageous effects on the hippocampus. Dreams can sometimes be prophetic and provide clues about health issues, prompting you to get the right checkups done. These type of clues and warnings if followed timely can prove to be lifesaving.

SPIRITUAL AWAKENING

Dreams can lead you to higher dimensions, can raise your consciousness when you experience an OBE (out-of-body experience), and can expose you to other hitherto unknown realms. Such experiences can dispel myths and fears of dying and leaving the physical plane. Travel through the astral world, and the recognition and realization of the power of the soul can transcend through ordinary limitations and lead to supremely beautiful, life-transforming experiences. A visitation from a dead relative can be a great source of solace, consolation, and peace and sometimes provides immediate remedies, as I have noted in one of my dream experiences. Your spirit guides and teachers may introduce themselves to you in dreams and guide you along your destiny. Knowledge of a past life can help solve current issues that seem troubling and can provide help and guidance to resolve them.

CREATIVE INSPIRATION

Several inventors, musicians, pioneers, authors, and others have referenced the influence of dreams as a source of inspiration and creativity. Robert Louis Stevenson, the famous novelist, is said to have relied on dreams to provide the material for his bestselling novels. In a way, dreams became the source of his livelihood. Just like many composers, scientists, and artists who have been inspired through the power of dreams to create spectacular works of art, songs, inventions, and products. Dreams are a sort of muse to inspiration, creating "Aha!" moments and epiphanies.

PREPARATION

Whether you are about to face an event the next day, month, or year, dreams prepare you for what is to come in a precognitive way. As the saying goes, "Forewarned is forearmed." Prior knowledge of an event in your life readies you for a fight-or-flight response, increasing the potential for survival and leading to the development of skills and techniques. In a dream I had just two days prior to a birthday celebration, the host of the party accorded me a rather lukewarm reception, which made me feel unwelcome. Following this dream experience, I had the choice to avoid attending this party, but I did attend since I wanted to confirm the dream as it appeared, and it was exactly so. Since I was anticipating such a reception, I was not disappointed. Had I not been forewarned in the dream, my sensibilities would have been hurt. On a more serious note, sometimes precognitive dreams can foretell a death. Death and dying are unpleasant, almost taboo subjects in our society. But a dream of a loved one crossing over provides the necessary time needed to deal with the actuality of death, almost in the manner of buffering the shock of departure.

WISH FULFILLMENT

Lucid dreams and astral voyages afford the opportunity of wish fulfillment. Whatever your heart desires, you can achieve it via the astral world. Visiting people or places, eating, drinking, sex, or socializing or any other activity can be activated through the etheric body, providing far-greater satisfaction and joy than in waking life. In fact, these voyages seem more real than reality. The higher the plane you travel to in the astral realm, the more intense the experience. As Leadbeater points out in his book *The Astral Plane,* everything exists in the Astral Plane, which can be visited almost as one does a foreign country.

ENTERTAINMENT

The fabulous voyages, especially in lucid dreams, the flora and fauna, the brilliant colors, and ephemeral creatures in dreams can be more fun than Disneyland. Imagine walking through a Jurassic Park–like setting along with elementals, the likes of which you have never seen before, while you experience the fantastic landscape, all the time in an invisible state, with no fear or phobias. Gliding through trees, hills, valleys, and other glorious landscapes can be so euphoric, you feel the joy for several days after. The joyous waterways, seascapes, bridges, and skies provide a fantastic panoramic backdrop for your very own set. In lucid dreams you can take control of the dream and pilot the plane in whichever direction you desire, since it can travel beyond the boundaries of the physical and rational. The options are unlimited. How fabulous is that. Lucid dreams enable you to overcome your fears by facing them head on, be it flying, sailing, mountain climbing, bungee jumping, or anything else. Even in a regular dream, scenarios that may seem ridiculous in daily life are presented in a humoristic, fun manner for your enjoyment.

PAST-LIFE RECALL

Besides regression techniques, past-life recall can be accessed through dreams. In dreams, you can travel forward or backward in time, thereby recalling a past-life experience that may prove useful in understanding and releasing blockages and negative patterns. You can learn to forgive someone when you recall a past life in which something played out to cause their hurtful behavior in this life karmically. Forgiveness lets you release trauma and pain that has been stagnating, blocking, and slowing down your spiritual growth. By viewing a past life, you can develop an awareness and understanding of how your current relationships may be influenced thus. Past-life awareness can lead to an "Aha!" moment of knowledge of karmic ties and explain the process of karmic balancing. You will begin to see a pattern in your present life and gain recognition and acceptance.

SELF-AWARENESS

One of the greatest benefits of dream recall and review is gaining knowledge about yourself. Akin to looking in the mirror to check your physical self, dreams educate you about your own psyche. By presenting the Anima/Animus, the Shadow, and other archetypes, dreams educate you and put you in touch with the most sacred part of the self. Things that you ignore during the day are brought to light at night, sometimes repeatedly in the form of recurring dreams. In this manner, dreams take on the role of psychotherapist, pointing to necessary changes in behavior or outlook. You can discover hidden talents hitherto unknown, giving you confidence that can lead to the development of a new hobby or profession. Skills that are latent can come to the forefront in dreams, encouraging and motivating you. This encouragement can lead to necessary change. As you change, so do your dreams.

DEVELOPMENT OF PSI

Also known as intuitive ability and other esoteric modalities, *PSI* is an all-encompassing term used to cover a broad range of paranormal phenomena. Things such as clairvoyance, clairaudience, claircognizance, and more are stimulated, developed, and enhanced for a better understanding of life. Dreams help you connect with the higher dimensions or, as some say, the "*inner planes*" of reality to receive clear mental guidance. Other information and guidance are enhanced from within rather than from without. Abilities such as telepathy and remote viewing can prove valuable and informative. Automatic writing can also be activated first in dreams, where clairaudient abilities facilitate this process by making you more attuned to higher centers. Several singers such as John Lennon, Paul McCartney, Eric Clapton, and even Mozart received their inspiration in this manner. Though not a composer myself, I choreograph workout routines to music in my dreams. This ability comes in very handy when I am rushed for time and facing a deadline.

OVERCOMING ADDICTIONS

Through astral travel, you can visit any place, do any activity you like, and gain more pleasure than you do in waking life. If food, drink, or any other substance poses a problem of addiction in your life, you can convert it to the dream sphere. By traveling astrally, you can eat, drink, or smoke without harming your physical body. At will, I travel to the best *patisseries* in Paris and order anything I want. I even have a conversation with the owner or other customers as I enjoy my pastries. All this with zero calories added. My husband, who was a chain-smoker for many years, one day decided to quit. He tried a few remedies to no avail. Then, I suggested the astral travel method of smoking in another realm. He struggled with it at first, but he started traveling in the astral realm whenever he had the urge to smoke and thereby fulfilled his desire. After a few months of this, he completely rid himself of this desire to smoke and has never touched a cigarette in twelve years. The best part of this was that it cost nothing, just a little patience and practice.

Dreams can be magical, mystical, thrilling, and entertaining as well. Even nightmares or other unpleasant dreams occur for a reason—the reason being primarily to help you navigate this journey called life.

Precognitive Dreams

Precognitive dreams are those which are self-fulfilling. Literally, dreams that come true. Precognitive dreams are fascinating but also the most difficult dreams to distinguish from other kinds, because they are like 20/20 vision. Most of the time, you don't know they are precognitive until after the event. They occur mostly in the early hours of the morning, when your REM cycle is the longest. If you see faces or places, you will remember them in detail the next day. The action in the dream may at first appear to be somewhat weird or bizarre, but of course it is only when the time that we experienced arrives in our present dimension that it make sense. Sometimes they are so startling and vivid that you wake up during the night. And if it happens to be an uncomfortable one, or something you might like to forget, you fall back asleep, and lo and behold, you have the same dream again! This is the way your subconscious brings your attention to the matter. This is a definite sign that some aspect of this dream will occur in your waking life.

When you recall your dreams, pay attention to the lighting. This is of particular significance. If a dream is brilliantly colored and very vivid, it reflects the superconscious state—the more evolved and heightened areas of consciousness. These types of dreams are nearly always prophetic. As always, in a dream it is important to note your feelings and emotions. Were you happy, sad, joyful, anxious, or just enjoying the ride? Making a note of your feelings and perceptions is extremely helpful when you have recurring dreams. Emotions in a dream can play a decisive role in discerning the crux of a dream.

One way to distinguish precognitive dreams is when they recur in a short time span, within the week or a few months. Also, if there is a commonality in the dreams. If you have the same person, event, or action coming up in frequently recurring dreams, this could be a clue that some aspect of this dream will occur in the future. Yet another way a precognitive dream presents itself to you is when extraordinary objects or images seem to send a definite message: for example, when you see an image or an object in a dream that seems quite unusual or strange. Many years before I entered the field of acting, I had a very striking dream in which I was walking on a broad street that covered several blocks, looking for the entrance to a particular building. As I was walking, I noticed what appeared in my dream state to be a large steel cage that was moving up and down. I could not find the entrance to that building, and I entered this large cage-like container.

Fast-forward a few years later, when I got cast to play an inmate in the Netflix series *Orange Is the New Black*. It was the very first episode of the first season. I took the subway to Long Island City, New York, and started walking along a broad street looking for the entrance to Kauffman studios. The entrance was not to be seen. I then noticed what looked like a freight elevator, made of solid steel on the inside as well. Someone opened the shutter of the elevator, which overlooked the street, just like in my dream! Noticing a person there, I inquired if it was building I was looking for. He said it was, and offered me a ride in the elevator, which connected to the other side of the building, where the official entrance was, with revolving doors, leading to a lobby. This is an example of a precognitive dream in which the strange object, the cage of my dreams, was exactly as it appeared. As you can see, something that could be passed off as just strange and meaningless was essentially beneficial in guiding me to my destination. Taking the cue from the dream of the cage-like structure, I used the dream clue and entered it instead of walking around wasting time. One important fact about reporting to a film set is that you can always be early but never late on set. There is an inside joke called "*Hurry up and wait*."

If your recurring dreams occur within regular intervals—for example, if the second one is within a few days and the third and the fourth even closer, such as a few days or a week or so—that could be a sign of a precognitive dream that will manifest very quickly in waking life. This is one way of finding a timeline in such a dream. Here is an example. I had three dreams within two weeks of a young lady I know becoming pregnant. The fascinating part is that the latter two dreams developed progressively like a novel. In the very first dream, this young lady was pregnant. In the second one I saw what appeared to be a baby girl. She had striking physical characteristics, which I could clearly see. At this point I knew that I had to meticulously journal the details, as I started to feel the excitement that this could lead to something that could be validated later. In the third dream, the same baby girl was wearing a pink dress with pink booties. Excitedly, I called this lady and asked her if by any chance she was pregnant. Not only did she vehemently deny it, but she gave me a rather terse response that she was focusing on her career and therefore had no plans for a baby.

Well, about a week later, I received a phone call from this lady, who told me she took a pregnancy test soon after our conversation (maybe to prove me wrong), and, much to her shock, she was indeed pregnant! Of course, the rest as they say is history. She went on to have a beautiful baby girl.

There are precognitive dreams, sometimes of a serious nature, which seem to prepare you a few years in advance of an event to occur, emphasizing the importance of recording and reviewing your journal every few months and years. I was having a series of dreams where I was in a hospital, being anesthetized, wheeled into the operating room, and other related events. These dreams were noticeably clear and repetitive. I was in the prime of health when I had these dreams and thought nothing of it, though I made my medical checkups a priority. Almost four years later, I was diagnosed with an aggressive form of cancer, which fortunately was detected at an early stage due to my diligence. What followed were many hospital visits and surgeries just like the dream foretold. As humans, we love to hang on to the positive dreams of winning the lottery or some such success. When our dreams warn us of an impending health condition or disaster, we tend to brush it off, hoping that it will disappear if we ignore it. But dreams always convey a message, preparing you if a shock is on the way. As in this case, precognitive dreams may take a few years to unfold, but unfold they do.

In a similar vein, some precognitive dreams can be more serious or worrisome. To illustrate an example of an unpleasant prophetic dream, the famous author Ann Rice comes to mind. In one of her speeches, when asked what inspired her to write *Interview with the Vampire,* Ann Rice referred to one of her dreams in which she saw her young daughter dying of a blood disease. Soon after this dream, her daughter was in fact diagnosed with leukemia and died. While grieving for her loss, she rapidly wrote the novel in record time of about three weeks, almost like a cleansing for her soul. The book was later made into a phenomenally successful Hollywood film, starring Brad Pitt and Tom Cruise, in which blood was highlighted. In my observation, seeing blood in dreams sends an extraordinarily strong message depending on the context.

Abraham Lincoln was known to be highly intuitive and himself believed in the power of dreams. After the death of his premature son, he often had conversations with the departed soul, which eased his pain, while his inconsolable wife struggled with her grief and consulted endless psychics. In fact, Lincoln foresaw his own death in a dream, weeks before he died. He had a dream in which he saw himself in a coffin in his own house. Upon asking a security guard who this was, he heard him reply that it was the president. Evidently, he was very uneasy about this dream, and although he did not admit this publicly, this dream came to pass ten days later.

In rare cases, when you have a precognitive dream, you know it instantly. You really do not have to ponder much or review it repeatedly to assimilate it. You do not even have to wait for time to tell the story and validate it. You experience an immediate sense of knowing that is definite and sure. There can be no room for doubt. This is the sleeping version of regular claircognizance, which is the ability to know something through a gut feeling or instinct—a feeling of total certainty of the accuracy of this information. It may come in a flash, like the panic of a mother who senses her child is in danger. Or it may come from the Higher Self as a direct message, like a feeling you know that something for sure is going to happen. It is even more rare, though not impossible, to be able to decipher the exact time span than an event will occur in a dream. A classic example is that of Calipurnia, the wife of Caesar in Shakespeare's illustrious play *Julius Caesar*. Calipurnia dreamt that all the Roman senators and statesmen were surrounding a statue of Julius Caesar that was shaped like a fountain and flowed with blood instead of water. All the Romans were enjoying this spectacle as they washed their hands in this blood. Terrified by this nightmare, she pleaded with him to stay home the next morning, but he ignored her fears and was assassinated.

Immensely important in distinguishing precognitive dreams is observing color. When you have recurring dreams in which the color remains constant, while other aspects, objects, actions, or events may be different, pay attention to the color. Color plays a significant part in our health and well-being. So many aspects of color are integrated into our body and mind: our endocrine system, physiology, psychology, feelings, emotional state, moods, even likes and dislikes and preferences. We even use colors to describe our state of being and our joy or sorrow. We often say things like, "I'm feeling blue" or "I'm turning green with envy" (although few will admit this). Or "I'm in the pink of health." If a certain color appears in your dreams repeatedly within a short period, it may indicate some event, action, or geographical location that corresponds to that particular color.

What follows are some interesting precognitive dreams that are actual cases.

GREEN, GREEN, GREEN

Here is an example of a dream I had in which the color was highlighted. I was dreaming on a regular basis for a couple of months where something in the dream was the color of green. There were more than a dozen dreams with green objects of different sizes. These objects ranged from a pair of shoes to something that looked like a mythic creature. Interestingly, the size of the object in the dreams progressively increased with time. Toward the end of this "green dream" period, the huge mythical creature repeated itself as the grand finale. When I recorded these dreams in my journal, there were no words to describe or name this gigantic, colossal creature that had no definite shape. After spending a great deal of time doing online research on prehistoric animals, my hopes of finding a match proved fruitless. Nothing quite matched the exact shape and shade of green that I saw so clearly in the dreams. Being an artist with extensive shades of paints and pencils, I drew the image and colored it. After these dreams came to an end, I was suddenly invited to an impromptu trip to visit the Nilgiri Mountains in the south of India. As we meandered our way through the winding roads and uphill climbs, I was stunned to see the green mythical creature of my dreams. The green mountains were shaped and sloped just like in my dream. Here the green mythical creature of my dreams was these enormous mountains, with little tea bushes circling them. An important point to make here is to use art to record your dreams. If something in a dream is obscure or inexplicable, make an illustration of it in your journal. Sometime in the future the image will prove meaningful.

THE GRAND THEFT

One night I had a dream in which a theft had taken place in my sister's home. It was a very clear dream in which I noticed that sizable amounts of valuable jewelry were taken out of the house. At the time I was estranged from my sister for more than two decades. I had no contact with her whatsoever. My dad was the go-between, providing information to both sides like a middleman. I knew that she had recently moved into a very large, grand home, with an enormous staff of helpers. Being more than 10,000 miles away, I had not visited my family in India for the last ten years. I therefore had no idea about the staff that worked in the house, or any other details. As soon as I possibly could, I relayed the information about the dream of the theft to my dad, who I assumed would pass it on to my sister, with the hope that she could heed the warning and avoid it. There is an almost ten-hour time difference, so by the time this message was received, the theft had already taken place. My dad was shocked at the development as he informed me about the event. He then asked me if I knew who the culprits were. Having no clues about the thieves from the earlier dream, I decided to go back, to reenter the same dream to find out more information. Prior to sleeping one night, I asked for information about the people involved in the robbery. This is what I saw in the dream, that it was not done single-handedly by one individual. Rather, it was a team of people, a couple. One who worked outside the home and one who worked inside the home.

The other clue I received was that this couple spoke a language that was different from the rest of the help. Excitedly, I called my dad and relayed this discovery. Much to my disappointment, no one could piece this information together, and the matter was forgotten.

However, giving up is not in my repertoire. My opportunity to crack this case (I know I sound like a sleuth) came a year later, when I finally was healthy enough to make that long, tedious, almost twenty-four-hour journey to visit my family. Although I stayed in my dad's house during my visit, I could see the daily goings-on in my sister's home across the street, and the activities of the staff, who also visited my dad. Thus, they were very much in my view, and I noticed that there was a husband-and-wife pair who spoke a different language than the rest of the staff did. The husband worked as the chauffeur, and the wife as the maid-in-waiting to my sister. This is important to note because it gives you an idea of how closely she monitored my sister's belongings, which gave her the best access to the jewelry. Bingo! Here was the couple, who managed to deftly smuggle jewelry from the inside of the home to the outside in teamwork fashion, leaving no room for suspicion. This is how you can reenter a dream to find missing information or fill in the blanks to any theme in your dream that seems incomplete, and to help put the missing pieces of the puzzle together. Of course, this takes practice, but it can be done.

DREAM DATE

Often, precognitive dreams are more direct in the message they convey. You do not necessarily have to read between the lines or wind your way through the symbolism of the metaphors. This dream recounted to me by a friend is a good example of one of those dreams that are simple to read like ABC. In the dream she saw a man with cornflower-blue eyes, playing a guitar. Shortly thereafter, she met a man with the same shade of blue eyes as those in her dream. It turned out that he was an ardent guitar player too! Evidently, she literally met the man of her dreams. They started dating and had a whirlwind romance. Although the relationship did not last, since he was not her type, because of the dream she went out of her comfort zone. She took a risk, put herself out there, and experienced something to help her in her search with a more discerning approach to figure out what she really was looking for in a relationship. The dream encouraged her to take a leap and try out an experience that would educate and enlighten her about her own preferences and help her in making the right choice.

THE THEATER

This was a dream I had that occurred after 7:00 in the morning, since I woke up around 5 a.m. and fell back asleep. In this dream, I was in a theatre/studio dressing room, which was like a rehearsal space. After completing the audition, I was selected for the role. Yay! We were doing a dress rehearsal. Two women were done playing their part, had changed, and left. There were two other women awaiting their turn along with me, as we waited to be called onstage for our segment. A few weeks after this dream, I auditioned and booked the role of a psychic in a short comedy titled *A Box of Ashes* in an off-Broadway playhouse. The story was comical and really brought in the "Ha-has" just as advertised. Like in the dream, there were a couple of other short plays as well to be showcased the same night as a compilation. We did have a few rehearsals, and a technical rehearsal, where I waited while the others finished their play just as the dream suggested. Early-morning dreams like this have a high probability of coming true.

DAD

A couple of years before my father passed away, I had regular dreams of him dying. At first, my thought was that these dreams were just a reflection of my anxiety and worry (since he lived almost 10,000 miles away). No one likes to face unpleasant things even in a dream, especially when it comes to family. Subjects such as separation, divorce, death, ill health, and loss of any kind, however inevitable, are quite repugnant. We do our best to avoid and evade them as much as we can.

But the consistency and recurring nature of this dream, in which my dad was dying, forced me to face the truth. Uncomfortable as this was, I started to slowly accept what was to come. As the months went by, my dreams painted the picture in more detail. This caused quite a dilemma for me, since I felt obligated to warn the other family members. But how does one approach this sensitive topic? As I was debating this in my mind, I had a dream in which my best friend's dad (who is on the other side) came and told me very definitely that my dad needed to get his passport ready soon. This was the impetus I needed to inform my family about the forthcoming event and gave me a clue of the time span (a passport/visa is generally required for an imminent journey). Feeling the urgency, therefore, I mustered up the courage to inform them. They were at first incredulous but cognizant of my prophesying abilities, so they understood that we all needed to prepare for this.

Three months later, my dad passed away. Soon after the funeral, I had a dream in which a very close high school friend whom I had lost touch with after high school phoned me to offer her condolences. Since we live on separate continents, she could not have had any information of the event of my dad's passing. We had no friends in common either. This seemed rather impossible; nevertheless, it felt good to connect with her even if only in a dream. Some months later, when I logged into my Facebook account, I saw a friend request from this very same friend! She was unaware of my dad's passing. After I informed her about it, she penned a meaningful message that was so beautiful and heartwarming. This is a great example of sympathetic dream telepathy in action. The symbol of a passport in a dream alludes to a distant journey, in this case of a spiritual kind.

THE GREEN LIGHT

As the release date of my second publication was approaching, I was wondering what day would be optimal to announce it publicly. According to my sales director, the release date was pushed back a month due to the COVID-19 pandemic. Darn! I waited so long and now this. However, I got over my initial disappointment, and before I went to bed that night, I asked the Universal powers for some advice and guidance on this matter. This is the dream I got. I was sitting in the back seat of a car, along with two other people. The door and window of the car were wide open. I know that sometimes you leave the window down, but no one ever leaves a car door open, right? Not usually. The three of us were engaged in a conversation, while my attention was suddenly drawn to the open space to my left by the open door. A little baby elephant walked by, stopped directly by us, waved his trunk in a happy fashion (elephants are known to have a temper), and walked off. I woke up the next morning, happy as a lark, realizing the elephant in my dream represented Ganesha (the Hindu god of astrology) who is half man and half elephant. Fittingly, the elephant happens to be on the front cover of my publication! Folks, this is NOT a coincidence—it is divine guidance. Whatever your beliefs or faith may be, trust in their power to guide and help you in life. The importance of paying attention to the signs in your way, and being open to receiving them, is paramount.

Although there was roughly more than a month to go for the fulfillment date, taking my dream as the green light to my query, I announced the details of my soon-to-be-released oracle deck, *The Mahabharata Oracle*. What happened next is unbelievable, and I still have goose bumps relating it. Two days later, I received a phone call from the publisher's marketing department, who informed me that the original release date was back in play. Wow! I went from on to off to on again.

Here is a brief explanation of the symbolism in my dream. The open door of the car in the dream signifies what occurred. A door that was supposed to be closed is OPEN, which explains the on-again/off-again scenario. There you have it. Then it all came together and made perfect sense. The bottom line is that you will get the answers you seek; you must just learn to trust.

THE MYSTERIOUS CHARGE

This dream occurred in the early hours of the morning. A man entered the bedroom as I was sleeping. The bedroom in the dream looked exactly like the one in my house (it is rare to see any part of your house in a dream as it appears in waking life). It was quite dark. This man went over to the left side of the bed, where my husband sleeps. I could not feel the presence of my husband in bed, so I figured he was probably downstairs. He usually rises before me. Then the intruder, who was still in the bedroom, talked on his own cell phone in a foreign language, which for some reason put the word Egypt in my head. All this while I was huddled underneath the covers. After I thought he left, I went downstairs, where my husband was sitting in his spot on the couch. I asked him what the intruder took, and he replied very nonchalantly that he took the car. I said, "Your car?!" My husband said, "Yeah, it was an old car anyway." And that was the end of the dream.

Later that morning, my husband was checking our bank statement online, as he is wont to do, and asked me if I had placed an online order in the amount of $60. I replied in the negative. He seemed unperturbed and said, "Oh well, let us wait and see what it is." The next day, there was a box from an online retailer on the front porch. I opened it to find some earphones, barrettes, and some meaningless items. There was no packing slip, no order form, nothing. This was most definitely no order of mine. Immediately I logged in to my online account, and there was no order transaction, no shipping information or address, again nothing. I called the retailer and explained the situation, emphasizing that I had not placed that order. The customer service representative said there was nothing she could do about it. She said that this type of transaction happens all the time, and informed me that I needed to cancel my credit card. Really? I was incredulous! Unfortunately, my husband spent a whole month fixing the issue—it was that complex.

There is a whole chapter in this book on interpreting dreams. However, I would like to enumerate some keys to interpretation with this example, which I often use in my workshops. Here are the clues.

- Early hours: generally a prophetic indication
- Quite dark: the dreamer is literally in the dark about the situation.
- Location near husband: he is also involved.
- Foreign language: It is very unusual to hear sounds as in noise, speech, or music.

Being highly clairaudient as a child, it is an ability I have. In this instance, the foreign language indicates someone or something foreign.

- The word "car" is a metaphor for card, as in credit card.
- The word "old" reflects the credit card, which was an old one and was in my husband's name.

If you put all the clues together, you can weave the result of what happened. The event occurred suddenly as if it came from left field. This was also the first time I experienced an online theft of this kind, which could have originated in a foreign country or by a foreigner. My husband said someone took his car, which fits the card being stolen for the transaction. He also described the car as being old, which again fits the attribute of the actual credit card.

RECONNECTING WITH AN OLD FRIEND

In this dream, I had a visit from Freida, the mother of an old high school friend whom I lost touch with after high school. She came by herself, bearing me a big envelope on which her family name was written in bold letters. Inside the envelope were items that were not exactly new, but rather leftovers that seemed to belong to some other person or establishment. The package contained several art and craft implements such as pots of paint, scrapbooking paper, little tins of linseed oil, watercolor pads, brushes, and a host of little things all bunched together that looked well worn and used. They were all items of use to me as an artist, representing things that bring me joy since I love to create.

Looking at the variety, I was both amazed and impressed by the thoughtfulness of this lady, whom I used to fondly refer to as aunt. Although this was a colorful, happy dream, I could make nothing of it.

A few months later, I received a phone call from Texas, from someone who said their neighbor was desperately trying to contact an old high school friend, and could it be me. She verified my name and high school and revealed that while the neighbor was searching through online accounts, she was helping her by making phone calls. Imagine her surprise when I confirmed her information. Very soon, my high school pal and I were reconnected, and we continue to share old memories and many conversations, including some with the mother who appeared in my dream. My friend elaborated on how she was desperately searching for me for some time, and how her mother was hoping and praying for her daughter's wishes to manifest. Apparently, a lot of people were involved in the search, and to my mind the mother's heartfelt desire was what activated it into reality.

A little explanation of symbology here is that the items in the dream were not new; they were old. That refers to the "old" friend. The art-and-craft supplies refer to the playtimes we shared as children, happy childhood memories that we continue to revisit and regale on an ongoing basis.

INSURRECTION IN THE CAPITOL, JANUARY 2021

In this dream, I was looking for a specialty store in an outdoor shopping area. I kept entering this lane but could not find the specific store. I gave up and left, and driving in my car I saw young Caucasian soldiers, all lined up. They were bare from the waist up, with camo pants. They had serious expressions, almost reflective of Auschwitz. But we were riding along Philadelphia and New Hope, in Pennsylvania, nowhere near Germany or Austria. I saw a huge building made to look old, which was a beer place. The whole dream reflected Germany, with an undertone of Philadelphia. There were barracks, barbed wire, and soldiers roaming about in army trucks. This was the dream I had on December 10, 2020. Following this dream, I made a vlog on my YouTube channel describing the dream. On January 6, 2021, there was an insurrection at the Capitol building in Washington, DC, where rioters illegally entered the building, causing havoc, death, and destruction. Some of the rioters were shirtless, wearing camouflage patterns and displaying Nazi-like tendencies. Once all these disturbances settled and order was replaced, some 50,000 troops were deployed in and around Washington, DC, leading to the presidential inauguration. There was a contingent of marines from Philadelphia who were called to the Capitol. On the news channel, I saw images of young troops, army trucks, and barbed wire, just as in my dream. As more details emerge from the investigation of the Capitol rioters, it has come to light that one of the rioters was in the habit of sporting a Hitler-style mustache to work.

WAR 2022

I made a YouTube vlog of a dream I had in December 2020. There were many elements and symbols in the dream depicting conflict between nations and outright war. This was a very clear dream, which prompted me not only to record it in my journal, but also to record it on video, which I did. On February 24, 2022, the Russian leader, Vladimir Putin, declared war on Ukraine, sending troops and waging a military battle. To view my vlog, visit my YouTube channel, @GitaRash.

Dream Your Reality

Alexander "the Great" had a remarkable dream one night. From the account of Plutarch, the Greek biographer, "Alexander chanced one night in his sleep to see a wonderful vision; a gray-headed old man. . . appeared to stand by him and pronounce these verses: 'An island lies, where loud the billows roar, Pharos, they call it, on the Egyptian shore.'" (Plutarch, "Life of Alexander," about 79 CE).

In this prophetic dream, the man was Homer, Alexander's favorite author. Even the place Pharos was familiar to Alexander from another of Homer's poems, "The Odyssey": "Out of the sea where it breaks on the shores of Egypt rises an island from the waters: the name men give it is Pharos" (Homer, "*The Odyssey*," written ca. 750 BCE; Book 4, about lines 354–55).

As an extremely ambitious man, young Alexander had lofty goals and aspirations of conquering the world. This was a highly detailed dream in which the location was named, described, and specified. Alexander followed the counsel given in this dream and established a port city on the island of Pharos, which became a vital part of his empire, which he renamed as Alexandria. Today, Alexandria is the second-largest city in Egypt. Alexander had several such dreams that appear to be precognitive in nature and acted as a precursor to his success.

Our mind is the most marvelous gift we are given, which we tend to underuse to a large extent. Equipped with such an infinite source of information and resource, there are many ways to unlock this treasure chest. We do use our conscious minds rather actively during the day, for pretty much every activity we are involved in.

Whether physical or mental, our minds are constantly engaged in a sometimes mindless chatter. But what happens to the other important details that we ignore for various reasons? They do not evaporate into thin air, just like that. These important little details are stored in your subconscious mind to remind you that they need attention. Until you work on them, they will keep reminding you through your subconscious in your dreams.

DREAM INCUBATION

Dream incubation has been practiced by many ancient cultures around the world. It was regarded as a very sacred ritual, which included elaborate preparations to prepare the dreamer. Dream incubation is said to have originated in ancient Assyria and Babylonia. In Egypt, it was almost a godly experience, highly revered and venerated, and was believed to have produced information and knowledge that led to many cures for illnesses and medical conditions. The famous Oracle at Delphi pronounced dream interpretations and even dispensed medical advice at the Temple of Apollo. All the way back in 1400 BCE, the presiding high priestess known as Pythia was highly respected by kings and commoners alike. In our time we have Edgar Cayce, also known as "the sleeping prophet," who used to put himself in a trance state and dictate to his secretary many cures, diagnoses, and medical treatments and other relevant information for clients who came to see him. These documents have been recorded and stored at the Association for Research and Enlightenment (ARE) center in Virginia, a nonprofit organization founded by Cayce, and are said to be astonishingly accurate.

According to Dr. Deirdre Barrett, a Harvard dream researcher, a large percentage of people can successfully find solutions and ideas practicing dream incubation, where the dreamer asks a specific question before going to sleep. As a recipient myself, I have received much guidance and advice through dream incubation, including solutions to problems, answers to questions, and profound messages from the spirit world.

PERSONAL DREAMS

In one dream, I was on the water in a big ship. I was walking on the deck at the side of the ship, came to a halt, and gazed at the water. The waters were calm, and the ship was sailing smoothly. There were two other people standing to my left, and I heard numbers being called on the public speaker. It was time to disembark, and I did so. Although I was on the edge of the water, as I left the ship I felt no fear!

Following the dream described above, I had another one, revolving around water. This time I was riding in a car on the edge of a sea. I could see the coastline and the sand, as the water weaved in and out. The driver in the car was my mom, who was driving rather fast and uninhibitedly (much to my surprise, since my mother was a very conservative driver). Safely, Mom weaved the car in and out of the water.

The two dreams described above changed my whole life from a vacation perspective. I had always wanted to ride in a boat, set sail on a ship, go on a sea voyage, and indulge in many other water-related things. As a child, I had a severe reluctance almost bordering on fear of water. I never learned how to swim and looked longingly at my friends who seemed to enjoy splashing around in swimming pools and playing fun games in the water. I had a sensitive middle ear that was prone to infections, and my mother was extremely cautious with me being around water. The rest of my family were adept swimmers, which made it even worse for me, since I felt inadequate and helpless. Growing up as a child, I felt like I was missing a very joyful activity.

In adulthood, I craved going on a cruise especially when I would hear the wonderful experiences of friends and coworkers. The thought of visiting different islands each day, docking in and out of ports while sleeping, sounded amazing. I really did not want to miss more fun that I could experience. However, my physical condition with the ear only deteriorated through time and nagged me every time I dared to fantasize about a cruise. Anyway, I decided to take a chance, since life is short, and prepared mentally to ride the seas. Turning on my dream drive, I first asked my mother for guidance, since she always protected me, and then started meditating on a cruise-fulfillment dream. As the proverbial saying goes, "Ask and you shall receive," I had a series of dreams that positively manifested in a cruise booking. In the second dream, as described above, it is my mother who is driving, which is not just permission but outright encouragement that the cruise would go successfully. Encouraged thus, with the guidance of my mother I went on my first cruise and enjoyed it thoroughly, taking many excursions as well, which involved traveling in much smaller boats and ferries from ports to land. Since then, I have taken several cruises fearlessly like the first dream suggests, being inspired by the actual dream.

We have seen many instances of how creators, inventors, and artists have been inspired by their dreams and imagination to manifest their goals. How do we apply some practices to achieve our goals and desires? Some of the ways are through positive thinking, active imagination, concentration, meditation, affirmations, visualization, mantras, and yantras. Practicing these must be regular and unwavering. If you really have a specific goal, be constant until you achieve it. A great way to begin is to set a definite time in the day, preferably before you go to bed at night. Use the time at your disposal to make a daily ritual of preparing for that exciting dream you are about to incubate. It does not matter if you have only fifteen minutes to devote each night; if you are regular, it will produce results.

Here are some of the key points to help you along this dream process. Intention and motivation are the key principles to successfully achieve the outcome you desire.

■ **Define your goal.** Have a clear vision of what it is you want. Fine-tune the details as much as possible. For instance, if you are desiring a house, visualize that house in detail, such as the style, size, color, and so on.

■ **Never give up.** Be persistent and consistent. Sometimes, it may seem like a long fruitless practice; some people may even discourage you, but stay committed to your goal, stay on the course.

■ **Believe in your power.** Have the confidence in your ability to create. YOU CAN CREATE. Your thoughts fly like winged birds to the universe, which deflects them back to you. Your thought must be strong so it can travel far. The definitiveness of a thought defines its clearness, and the clearness of a thought spells its outcome. The more one-pointed and focused your thought is, the farther it can travel.

■ **Have patience, do not set a time limit, refrain from "the Timeline" syndrome.** Let everything unfold as it should. Trust the universe for its timing. Bear in mind that what you seek is seeking you.

■ **Stay positive.** Do not let negative thoughts invade your practice. Some things do take longer to materialize. Trust your inner guidance and follow the flow of your energy, since it is aligned with the universe. Remember the universe is listening to you; when your energy flows along with the forces of the universe, it has a dynamic effect.

Practice one or more of the exercises described below to incubate your wish in your dream and manifest your reality.

Gratitude is twice blessed. Remember to acknowledge your dreams and wishes and offer gratitude with regularity.

MEDITATION

Choose a time of day when you can be undisturbed, preferably before going to bed at night. If you like to take a warm bath or shower, it will help relax you. Wear comfortable loose clothing that is convenient for you to sit or lie in a relaxed position. A candle or incense can provide good ambience. You may close your eyes in quiet solitude and count to ten if you need to. This can help hypnotize you and clear your mind of other thoughts. Stay well hydrated and take a few deep breaths to relax your body. Once you reach a state of relaxation, focus on your wish and silently communicate it to your subconscious mind. Remember your subconscious mind can take instruction from you like a student does from a teacher. You can even visualize the event in your mind's eye. Music is optional. Spend as much time as you need to.

MANTRAS

Sound is a powerful vibration that has been employed for several purposes since ancient times. Used in prayer, healing, and art forms such as singing and dancing, the energy of sound is said to transcend dimensions, and is an immensely powerful way of creating consciousness and contacting higher beings of energy. As an ancient meditative practice, sound is used in singing bowls, quartz bowls, and wind chimes to target healing and well-being of various parts of the human body and mind. The special hertz frequency of sound can bring about heightened states of consciousness and promote relaxation; the binaural beats promote altered states of consciousness and enhanced meditation. The sound of the conch, the drumbeat, ringing of the bell, chants, and mantras, be it Gregorian, Vedic, Buddhist or Islamic, are known to bring the body into a vibrational state of harmony and balance and induce states of deep trancelike experiences. There are several wonderful mantras and chants to choose from the plethora that is available today.

Find something that resonates with you if a sound meditation/relaxation method appeals to you. Once you attain a deep state of relaxation, allow your mind to focus on your goal, whatever it may be. Spend a few minutes in this meditative state until your subconscious receives a clear message.

KIRTAN

Kirtan is a powerful song/melody to connect with the very core of your being, right to your heart, and emanate it back to the universe. The music is melodious, joyful, and uplifting, and the ancient Sanskrit lyrics lend themselves to a peaceful state of meditation, inner peace, and transformation. Kirtan provides a powerful resonance to connect to the divine within the self and connect to others as well. This type of chanting does not require an intense focus, because the repetition of the rhythmic lyrics occupies your mind and leads you to a meditative state. For the beginner who is embarking on meditative practices, I highly recommend this.

Kirtan music is generated by an instrument known as a harmonium. Herein lies a synchronistic connection between the word "harmony" and the instrument "harmoni. . . um" (an amalgamation of the words *harmony* and *Om*). Also known for aiding in health and healing, kirtan chanting has numerous benefits, including emotional peace and happiness. Furthermore, it is an effortless, joyful way to create a state of bliss. Kirtan can be done in a group setting as well, for group therapy, distance healing, or plain energy sharing, to raise positive vibrations as a sort of communal invocation. For those who find it challenging to meditate, the kirtan is a perfect way to gradually start and train yourself to other methods that require a more serious focus. There are several (including Grammy Award winning selections) kirtans available from which to choose.

SACRED DRUMMING

The Native Americans believe that we all are born with a drum, our heartbeat, the rhythm of our body, which connects us with the truth of spirit and leads us to the universe. Invoking a deep trance and meditative state, drumming has been practiced by ancient cultures and is increasingly becoming popular now for healing, grounding, and attaining a state of peace and balance. In Haiti, drumming is used to connect with spirits called "loas," who are regarded as guides and helpers. In Native American, African, and other cultures, drumming is a sacred ritual practiced for several purposes such as healing, cleansing, purifying, and accessing areas of consciousness, communicating with ancestors, and achieving a trance state. Full-moon drumming circles have now become a part of our mainstream modern culture. Shamanic drumming classes and courses are available, as well as drumming music in different formats. If drumming is your beat, you can use this method to program your subconscious.

MANDALA

Mandala: a more traditional design of the Mandala (courtesy of Kamlesh Rajesham)

The Mandala is one of the most powerful methods of attaining focus and concentration to prepare your mind to access the cosmos. As you gaze into the center, at the dot, you connect with the innermost part of your being, your psyche.

You are looking at the completeness of the universe and drawing your attention to the perfect harmony of the yin and yang or Shiva and Shakti, the divine energy that guides and connects you with your higher self. Gradually, the left brain will be quieted, allowing the right intuitive side of the brain to flow freely. After a few moments of total focus, visualize your wish and empower your gaze with it directly onto the center, imprinting it subliminally.

YANTRAS

The Sri Yantra is a dynamic version of the mandala that engages your focus and energy to the very center or core, called Bindu. Designed with precise sacred geometry, the triangles and circles interlocking each other are specifically located to transport you to cosmic realms fearlessly. Clearing negative energies and fostering positive vibrations, this yantra is significant for wealth and abundance. If financial prosperity is your goal, this mantra is key. The meditation technique to follow with this yantra is described at the end of the chapter.

Sri Yantra

CHAKRA MEDITATION

Chakra meditation is a natural way to tune in to your body and energize the powerful vortices to flow more positively and align with harmonizing your wishes. These psychically potent energy centers can be activated to vibrate and establish your connection with the universe. Chakras are your portals to transformation and growth. Whether you are seeking spiritual enlightenment or material abundance, use the appropriate chakras to manifest your dreams accordingly. While it is important to have a harmonious, balanced chakra system overall for optimal health, you can further develop the solar plexus and third-eye chakras to strengthen intuition, astral powers, increased awareness, and other psychic abilities.

If you like to use crystals to enhance the chakra meditation practice, use the crystals associated with each chakra to energize the body and release blockages. Crystals help balance the electromagnetic field and have tremendous power over the body and spirit. You may be drawn to a particular crystal; use that as a guide. There are innumerable varieties of crystals and several versions of one crystal available as well. The lotus flower is an integral part of the chakra system symbolically. You can place a drawing or picture nearby of a lotus flower to inspire and guide you. Additionally, you can also chant or play a recording of the different sounds associated with each chakra, as mentioned in the chapter on dream drive.

MUDRAS

Mudra means a mark or a gesture referring to the hand, symbolizing a sacred, mystical gesture. Mudras are commonly used in yoga practices to channel and direct energy to the body in a fashion similar to that of chakras. The movements are not restricted to the hands; they can include the body as well. Mudras have been used since ancient times to balance and harmonize the flow of energy for physical well-being and mental and emotional peace, in addition to promoting deep relaxation and psychic abilities. The movements direct awareness and energy to the higher chakras, inducing a higher state of consciousness.

Hakini Mudra to manifest fortune

Each finger on the hand corresponds to the five elements: fire, air, water, earth, and ether. These fingers act as stimulants to activate the elements to balance the body.

The thumb corresponds to fire; the index finger, air; the middle finger, ether; the ring finger, earth; and the last finger, water. There are several combinations of mudras employing these ten fingers, which act as electric circuits to invoke a specific state of mind and forge a link to the cosmos. All ten fingers have individual meanings, which are in turn connected to the solar system and the cosmos. Accordingly, the right hand is considered to possess a more masculine influence represented by the sun. The left hand, representing the moon, is considered to reflect feminine energy. Likewise, each finger influences your life on the basis of its association with the different planets in the solar system. The thumb, corresponding to the element of fire, is also associated with the planet Mars.

In palmistry, a well-formed strong thumb indicates a strong, dominating personality. The index finger, corresponding to air, is associated with the planet Jupiter, representing knowledge, wisdom, and teaching. The middle finger, corresponding to the element of ether, is associated with the planet Saturn, representing control and restriction. The ring finger, corresponding to the element of the earth, is associated with the sun, representing light, life, energy, and vitality. The last finger, associated with water, represents the planet Mercury, which rules communications, change, business, and social media.

If you choose a mudra meditation for your dream incubation, assume a comfortable posture and select a gesture appropriate for that element. For instance, if you would like to be able to remember your dream by boosting your memory, you can do the Hakini mudra by touching the tips of the fingers of each hand to the opposite. Focus on the mudra and notice the effect on your body. There are many sources available describing the different mudras. Auras can also be seen by an effective mudra practice. Listen to your body for reading signs related to health and healing to enhance its manifestation. By adding an affirmation to a mudra, it expands to a powerful vibration, and the actualization of your dreams. Whatever your desired wish may be, select an appropriate affirmation to recite verbally or mentally to enhance the mudra movement.

The ancient Indians performed their meditation and devotional practices on a mat made of "kusha" grass. The kusha grass, also known as darbha or halfa grass, is said to possess the ability to block x-ray radiation and conduct phonetic vibrations through its tip. Even today, Hindu rituals are performed with a string of kusha grass tied to the forefinger as an access portal to the gods, almost like a wand. Kusha grass is also used in other rituals and sacred ceremonies such as house blessings to attract peace and prosperity and ward off evil effects. You can practice meditation with this "kusha" grass or even place it under your pillow at night to manifest clear, inspiring dreams. According to certain Buddhist texts, the Buddha attained enlightenment while seated on kusha grass under the bodhi tree. Due to the popularity of the kusha grass, mats and other products are widely available today. You can check out several stores online.

PICTURES, IMAGES, AND VISUAL AIDS

Visually focusing on an image of your desire sends signals to your subconscious mind as something of significance, which explains why nightmares can occur in dreams after watching horror films. This method works extremely well for desired trips and voyages. Feasting your eyes on images of sandy beaches, palm trees, or even the Egyptian pyramids or the Eiffel Tower can set the wheels in motion to manifest a desired voyage. As with other methods, this practice of viewing images, whether in magazines or electronically, needs to be done regularly.

The more you train your subconscious mind and imprint a desire, the greater the chances of success. In one of the actual dream manifestation examples, as described at the end of this chapter, the wedding dress in the closet was crucial to manifesting the desire of a wedding. If weight loss is your goal, draw a picture of yourself with the ideal shape you desire. Be realistic and choose a practical, achievable body shape. Gaze at this image every night before you sleep, thus reprogramming your mind to change your current diet/exercise lifestyle to achieve your desired goal. You can even indulge in the purchase of a piece of clothing in your ideal size and hang it in your closet.

Visualize yourself in this clothing before you sleep at night. I can assure you that this picture will occur in your dreams. When you experience the achievement of a goal in your dream, you get encouragement to take the right steps. Therefore, once you dream it, you will convert it to reality. This has worked for me. If you are patient, determined, and unwavering in your practice, the results will come.

If becoming a property owner is on your list of goals, keep an image of your ideal house, or even a small facsimile of a house in any material by your bedside as you practice each night, selecting any one of the methods that appeal to you. Watching a real-estate reality show or some other program highlighting homes before you go to bed at night will help reinforce the idea. Visualize yourself in the home of your dreams, picture your children in the yard, your pet on the porch, that large screen television to watch games or shows. Every little detail you focus on will guide you toward your goal.

As a young woman, I always fancied a red sports car. As a doodler, I created several drawings of a swanky red Corvette-shaped car. I pictured myself in the driver's seat, zipping past all the other cars on the highway. After a few months, I started having dreams of myself in a red car. Once I got my driver's license, my dad wanted to reward me for attaining outstanding educational achievement. He asked me to pick a car as a gift, and of course I got a red sports car. It can truly be said that this was not a case of "I never dreamt of it." Imagination is more important than willpower and acts as a key to achieving your goals.

MEDITATION ACCESSORIES

ESSENTIAL OILS

Widely popular in our society, aromatherapy as a holistic healing method is a multimillion-dollar business now. Understandably so, considering the innumerable benefits for the body, mind, and spirit. Made from plant extracts, essential oils have been used for centuries for therapeutic and aesthetic purposes, to name a few. Studies and research are ongoing for their effectiveness for other medical conditions such as the use of peppermint oil for headaches.

Ongoing clinical trials for anxiety, depression, nausea, and other conditions appear promising. Skin-care companies have been marketing essential oils used in creams and lotions to relax the muscles and release the tension. When inhaled, these essential oils travel from the nerves to the brain, having an impact on the emotional-center amygdala, or they can be applied directly to the skin. A warm bath with some drops of an essential oil such as lavender can also help soothe and relax the body in preparation for meditation. There are several varieties of essential oils as well as several qualities available today, along with a choice of tools such as aroma sticks. Not only do essential oils soothe, relax, and destress your body, they also are uplifting, help you sleep, and can be used for memory recall, especially of a past life. Odors are known to activate the pineal gland, elevating the dream experience and imagination. Try on different scents to see if anything resonates with you. Smell is a powerful sense that can trigger memories and emotions, can cause regression, and can help lead you to some profound information. In the context of a dream, a smell can act as a symbol to provide the core meaning. Intricately linked to the sense of smell is the sense of taste. Clairgustience, or the ability to psychically smell or get a taste of something, can very well be felt in dreams while asleep. Essential oils can evoke feelings of taste as well.

Here is a brief explanation of how these oils can be used. Essential oils are organically made from leaves, bark from trees, herbs, and rinds of fruits and vegetables. They have proven to be effective when used in the right way. A little knowledge is required to learn the proper way these oils can be administered. The oils when applied send chemical messages to the brain that can soothe tension and stress and cause calmness. There are several dos and don'ts to follow. Some oils need to be diluted with carrier oils. Generally, most of the oils aid in spiritual and meditative practice and are easy to administer. Oils such as frankincense are particularly helpful in grounding and forming spiritual connections. Lavender can improve memory and recall.

CRYSTALS

Crystals have been used since ancient times for their beauty and adornment, in health and healing, and in rites and rituals. They are becoming enormously popular today. Crystals are prized for their ability to heal mind, body, and soul. There are numerous crystals, each with its own variety, including grade, color, and cut. Mention has already been made of the use of crystals to enhance the flow and balance of chakras. Used in meditation, crystals can enhance many aspects of PSI and lead to a profound understanding of the universe. The blue quartz is an important

Amethyst: one of the most colorful crystals

crystal to enhance spiritual communication and acts as a psychic protector. Working with the energy of the throat chakra, this crystal can assist in enhancing dream experiences and astral connections.

RUDRAKSHA BEADS

"Rudra" is the name of Siva, and "Aksha" is said to be the eyes of Shiva. The ancient belief is that when Shiva pondered upon the world and the destiny of man, he shed tears of compassion. These tears upon falling on the earth transformed into trees that grow these brown, seedlike beads. They vary in size but are generally brown in color and round. Containing the elements oxygen, hydrogen, nitrogen, and carbon, these beads have potent benefits for the wearer, both medicinal and spiritual, and

Rudraksha Beads

are also known for curing psychosomatic illnesses. Wearing these beads promotes clarity and focus. Commonly worn as prayer beads, rudrakshas are highly prized and valuable. Traditionally the beads are strung in a necklace called a mala, which can be worn around the neck or around the wrist. The beads are 108 in number plus the Bindu. They also contain healing properties and protective power. Rudraksha beads promote self-awareness and calmness of mind and are a great tool when used in meditation. Lately these beads have become a popular and trendy fashion accessory both for men and women.

TAROT AND ORACLE CARDS

Oracle card to invoke Abundance

Tarot as a method of divination has existed for centuries. Used in games and fortune-telling, Tarot and oracle cards have gained in popularity over the years. The different suits in a Tarot deck represent elements such as earth, air, fire, and water. The Major Arcana helps you develop a richer and deeper relationship with higher beings. Full of symbology, brilliant colors, and images, both Tarot and oracle cards are a great source to invoke imagination and fantasy. They act brilliantly as a visual tool to embed images in your mind to inspire your dreams. Whether you perform a ritual before you lay your cards, or a silent meditation, select the appropriate images from the deck and gaze at them, with an intention, desire, or goal in mind that you would like to manifest.

EARLIEST DREAM MANIFESTATION

As a young child growing up in India, I yearned to travel all over the world, visit exotic places, explore different cultures, and live for some time in different countries. Geography was one of my favorite subjects in high school. I would pore over the world map and pinpoint my places of interest. I would make up addresses and post them as my residences, much to the amusement of my classmates. When asked what I wanted to be when I grew up, I used to respond that I wanted to be a diplomat. In my young mind, I thought that was the only way a person could travel and reside in many countries. After graduating from high school, I pursued the desire of getting a foreign degree. My heart was set on getting an MBA in the United States of America, much to the disappointment of family and friends, who saw no reason I could not just do it in India. Coming from a wealthy family, there was really no need for me to venture out and take risks. Back then, the process was not so easy or convenient as it is today. For one, there was no internet, no cell phone, not even email. Everything took time and depended on, yes, the snail mail.

The process of applying to American universities was expensive, tedious, and time consuming. The added complexity was procuring a student visa from the American consulate, which could be issued only after a document was provided of a secured admission and with solid proof of a well-padded bank account. To top this, the alternate means of communication was the phone, which was also an expensive means of communication internationally. To make matters more difficult, the ten-hour time difference between India and the US was yet another issue. While it was day in one country, it was after office hours in another. Sacrificing sleep to communicate with admission offices was another factor. Yet, I persisted and sent applications to many universities in just as many states, spending a great deal of money on nonrefundable application fees.

Despite having good grades and great SAT and GMAT scores, what ensued was a trying experience. For some reason or another, I didn't succeed in my attempts to secure admission for a long time. Although the experience was frustrating and exhausting, I never gave up. My sister was quite insistent that I just abandon the idea. This gave me the inspiration to imagine, visualize, and start dreaming about where I wanted to be. Once I decided that and started working on it, I started dreaming of a strange setting, where I was going in and out of classrooms with strangers and communing in a large dining space that overlooked a garden. There was a series of such dreams, and nothing that was noticeably clear. Until one day in a dream I saw snow, and myself in a heavy coat walking into a classroom.

By this time, it was almost two years since I had started what my friends referred to as "utter madness." Undeterred, I was even more convinced that my nightly dreams were going to come true. Of course, people around me thought I was a complete lunatic, and tried to persuade me to abandon my wild dreams and register into a good local university. My dreams after two long, frustrating years finally came true! One day, the mailman delivered my admission letter along with the invitation to apply for the required I-20 student visa. This was the last hurdle.

There was a rumor going around that only 50 percent of applications at the American consulate that issued these visas were approved. Therefore, this was not yet a done deal. My dad booked flights and made hotel reservations in another city where the American consulate was located. The consulate office opened at 9 a.m., but the waiting line started to form at 3 a.m. Early that morning, I got in line and chatted with the rest of the people, all of whom were hoping they were going to be in that list of 50 percent of approved visas. The interview itself was quite simple; the consulate officer approved my visa and told me I could pick it up after 3 p.m. that day.

I enrolled myself in the MBA program at a university in northeastern Pennsylvania, where snow is a prominent feature of the winter season. Another fascinating aspect of this whole process was why it took two years to manifest. To be honest, I never realized this myself until several years later. This is what transpired a few months after I started attending classes at the university. I met my husband on the same campus and got married a year later. Why is this significant? Because that was the "TIME" I was supposed to meet and marry whom the universe assigned to me.

Which is why it had taken two years, since this was the plan the universe was working on. In retrospect, had I secured admission before that assigned time, I would not have crossed paths with my future spouse-to-be. Or I would have been in a different school or state. This was destiny. The delay was a blessing in disguise and proves that whenever we desire something, we need to understand that there are several forces in play, most of them unseen and unknown by us. There is a larger plan, a higher hand directing the orchestra of our lives. Once we clarify what we want, the universe also gives us what we need.

THE FRENCH TEACHER

One of my friends, a French teacher, was at the time working in a college in a large city. Although she loved her job, she was starting to feel a little dissatisfied with her environment. As time went along, she was getting more restless and irritated. She shared her feelings with me about wanting to move to a completely new environment and was desirous of a new experience. I asked her if she had any school, city, or state in mind. She laughed and replied that it was something of a lottery to get a teacher's job; she explained that a position was generally available when a teacher retired or died. However, I encouraged her to pursue her dream and told her to first visualize a place and then start dreaming about it at night.

Although not fully convinced, she took my advice and excitedly reported that she was having dreams about being in a midsize idyllic town, where she felt very peaceful. She was still doubtful if this would ever materialize; nevertheless, she was savoring those visions.

This is what happened while she was still having her idyllic dreams on and off. In less than a month, she received an email from a colleague informing her about a teaching position that was becoming available in a small town. Apparently, the teacher in that school had accepted a teaching assignment in Europe, since she wanted a foreign experience, and therefore there was a need to fill the position she was vacating! See how the universe works!

THE ASPIRING BRIDE

On a teaching trip to Los Cabos, Mexico, I met a young lady who was the physical fitness coordinator at the resort I was staying and teaching at. The resort was very upscale with elite guests, beautiful interiors, and stunning vistas. As a guest instructor, I was treated like royalty and, given the best suite overlooking the Pacific Ocean. I instructed an eager, well-behaved group of people in a gorgeous, panoramic setting. This coordinator, whom I will refer to as Lydia, attended all my classes during the week. She developed an affinity for me and spent her free time hanging out with me and arranging special things such as cooking classes, for my enjoyment. We started having private conversations about our personal lives.

She confided in me about her concerns of being single. She really wanted to start a family and realized that her biological clock was ticking away. Even though she had dated a few colleagues at her workplace, nothing materialized. She even admitted to having purchased a wedding dress that she hung in her closet. I said that was a great beginning, and asked her if she had an idea of who her ideal partner could be. She replied that if he were a good person and a good provider, she would not be too picky. Great again. But then, there are innumerable people on this planet who could easily check those two boxes.

My advice to her was to make a detailed plan of who her ideal partner should be, including his physical features and other qualities that were important to her. Once that was done, I told her to visualize an image of this ideal man walking down the aisle with her, every night until she transported this vision to her dreams. At first, she had trouble remembering her dreams. She said they were just a blur with nothing concrete. I told her to keep at it and start journaling whatever she saw in her dreams. Then I asked her to place her wedding dress more conspicuously in her view and focus on it before she went to bed. She did this religiously every night. I received several emails from her, happily informing me that she was remembering her dreams, although there was still no aisle or church present in them. Almost a year later, I received an invitation from the same resort to spend a week as a guest instructor. The invitation came from the new manager of the resort, along with a wedding invitation to the ceremony with him and Lydia! I still have goose bumps as I write this. Don't we all love happy endings!

THE HAPPY CRUISER

One of my clients who had never been on a cruise was longing to spend a romantic voyage over the seas to take her romantic relationship to the next level. She was doubtful and hesitant, with a fistful of reasons and excuses about it ever panning out. Upon my advice she started a regular ritual before bedtime, which involved watching travel shows, and series such as *The Love Boat*. Although I knew her quite well, I knew nothing about her partner, except that his work took priority over everything else. For some reason, I was more excited than her, and for this cruise, waiting and watching to see the development. There was no news for a while, and I assumed his work took precedence, so I totally forgot about it. In the next Tarot reading she had with me, I could see an upcoming trip in her cards near water. At that point she burst out and shared the happy news that the cruise was booked, and her partner had taken some time off from work for the trip.

These are just a few examples of successful dream manifestation through the subconscious mind. Although there are many more I can list, these cases offer substantial evidence of how you can dream your reality.

Dream Drive

Dreams arise from the hard drive of your subconscious mind. Elaborate productions are created by this hard drive, while we sleep at night, to bring your awareness to what your conscious mind may have swept away during the day. All those experiences, events, and circumstances, even past-life memories that are stored in this hard drive, appear in full force almost like a staged play in your dreams. The subconscious mind is like a fascinating warehouse storing all kinds of props, costumes, and accessories that the conscious mind is unaware of, represses, or chooses to ignore. Even the future is embedded in the subconscious mind. Our bodies contain an abundance of energy, information, and potential. Within our physical structure lie multiple avenues, which can be tapped into to gain knowledge of dreams and enhance the capacity to activate the imagination and dreaming quotient. In a relaxed state, the subconscious mind can be activated to procure answers and solutions almost magically.

ASTROLOGY AND DREAMS

We are all in the gutter, but some of us are looking at the stars.
—Oscar Wilde, *Lady Windermere's Fan,* Penguin Popular Classics, 1995

The sky, the planets, and all other celestial bodies have fascinated humans since early times. There were several ancient cultures across the globe that started studying the various positions and aspects of the celestial bodies and developed an astronomical/astrological relationship with them, by making a connection with the innate nature of the human being. One of the earliest cultures to devise a mathematical formulation of the stars and planets was the early Indians seven thousand years ago. Known as Vedic astrology or Jyotish, this science was written in Sanskrit.

Several sages developed different versions of calculating a person's events in his lifetime on the basis of the picture of the sky when he was born. According to author K. Subramaniam, "Possibilities, probabilities, and conclusions arrived at by modern physics, astrophysics, biology and biochemistry in the recent past, has been discussed in Jyotisha Vidhya centuries before, long before Isaac Newton and Albert Einstein were born" (Subramaniam 1994). Although extremely complicated, Jyotish Vidhya is popular among Indians even today. In fact, no important event in life, such as marriage, is conducted without the consultation of a person's natal chart. Jyotish Vidhya is a sidereal-based astrological method that uses the moon's placement as the focal point in the natal horoscope.

Sometime in the sixth century BCE, the Greeks also evolved the Hellenistic system of astrology, linking human divinities to the Greek gods. The early Mesopotamians closely observed galactic patterns and even named the constellations in 3000 BCE. The Babylonians, who were notable astronomers, started to play around with the sequence of time and linked it to the movement of the constellations. Although astrology and astronomy coexisted on the same plane for some time, the further study of seasonal and celestial events led to its bifurcation, and they constitute distinct and separate disciplines today.

The zodiac was designed as the twelve specific constellations. At first, astrology was used to predict weather patterns for agricultural purposes, but it soon developed to include the forecasting of war and momentous events in human lives. The knowledge of astrology is still evolving, with the discovery of new planets, life on different planets, the energetical shift of the cosmos, and its impact on humanity, all leading to broad-based and widening theories.

Recently there has been an exciting new discovery in Egypt, in the Greco-Roman temple known as the Temple of Esna. During the restoration process of an ancient temple neglected and covered with soot, some carvings and inscriptions have been unearthed. These elaborate carvings depict constellations and cosmic images, connecting them to one called *Apedu n Ra,* translated to "The geese of Ra." Researchers have discovered beautiful original colors from two thousand years ago, along with novel inscriptions, even those of unknown constellations.

Prominently featured among these inscriptions is Ra, or the sun god, whom the Egyptians revered with the utmost sanctity. The ceilings of the temple are filled with celestial designs, including the Big Dipper, which they referred to as Mesekhtui, and Orion (Sah). The temple is surrounded by other buildings dating back to 1589. The process employed by the ancient Egyptians to decorate the temple was complex. The drawings were first created in black ink, then converted to reliefs and finally painted with colors. The ceiling, however, was not progressed from the inked stage and is being discovered only at this time.

Nostradamus, the sixteenth-century French astrologer, physician, and infamous seer and the author of *Les Propheties,* was so mesmerized by astronomy and astrology that he moved away from his medical training to pursue occultism. He went on to author almanacs and other works that attracted the attention of Catherine de Medici, wife of Henri II. She became his biggest fan. Having read subtle hints about threats to the royal family in his writings, she invited him to the royal palace and asked him to draw the horoscopes of her children. Enjoying her confidence and support, he was made counselor by Catherine and spent a great deal of time at the palace and was also appointed as physician in ordinary to the young prince, King Charles IX of France. He wrote the horoscopes of the seven royal children in the Chateau de Blois. When he was introduced to them at the Chateau de Blois, it was with trepidation in his heart that he greeted them, since he had already predicted some ominous events for them in his writings. By the way, if you ever visit France, a trip to the Loire River valley is a must, as is a visit to the Chateau de Blois, with its octagonal staircase and several gardens and loggias all styled in Italian Renaissance architecture. Should I say *magnifique*?

In his writings, Nostradamus cleverly disguised his predictions in the form of quatrains (rhymed four-lined verses) to avoid heresy and the Inquisition. His almanacs and predictions for the coming year became popular with farmers and the public in general, increasing his popularity and bringing him more fame, making him one of the notable figures of the Renaissance period. Although he was criticized by some contemporary colleagues, he continued to compose several quatrains about mundane events such as droughts, battles, plagues, famine, floods, and other natural and man-made disasters. His writings are still popular today, as they were in the past, and he is credited with many world predictions, such as the French Revolution, the rise of Napoleon and Hitler, the assassination of American president John F. Kennedy, the great fire of London, and even the 9/11 attacks on the World Trade Center. The world continues to be fascinated by this medieval seer and even credits him with the prediction of the COVID-19 pandemic. An analysis of the natal chart of Nostradamus is provided at the end of this chapter to depict his oracular powers. Please note that sidereal astrology uses a square-shaped chart, not a circular one.

What were the "Prophesies" based on? According to Nostradamus, it was based on "judicial astrology" and the tracking of planetary alignments and configurations, comparing them to past events, and divining the future. Every night when the family slept, he used to retire to his study on the top floor, where he gazed at the stars and observed the omens until the wee hours of the morning. He also used a scrying method to foresee events as he meditated and went into a trance. All the information he gathered he promptly recorded in his diaries. In his own words, he says, "When I am seated alone at night in my secret study, musing over the brass bowl which rests on a tripod, a slender flame comes forth from nothing and signals the time for me to utter a sacred mantram. With divining branch in hand its wet lip points to limb and foot. Then my hand trembles and, overcome by awe, I await. Heavenly Splendor! The Divine Genius is present" (*Les Propheties Michel de Nostredame, 1557*).

The tripod has an interesting history; it was depicted by ancient Greek artists as representing the god Apollo. In fact, the priestess also known as the Oracle (Pythia) sat on a tripod in the temple at Delphi and pronounced dream interpretations and relayed other psychic information channeled through Apollo, like a medium. Modern metaphysicians place the crystal ball on a little tripod and gaze into it for divinatory purposes. The magic cauldron is also either placed above a tripod or hung below by a tripod.

In modern times we have Jeanne Dixon, an astrologer, seer, and regular columnist in *Parade* magazine, who accurately predicted the assassination of John Kennedy. Her quote "Armageddon will come in 2020 when the false prophet Satan and the antichrist will rise up and battle man himself" (Dixon 1972) can be loosely interpreted to mean the devastating effects of the coronavirus in 2019–21. Joan Quigley, another modern astrologer, rose to fame as the personal advisor in the White House to Nancy Reagan. Joan had apparently given a lot of advice on several matters, including politics and the timing and planning of President Reagan's daily activities. Joan's position as advisor to the Reagans brought her fame and success, leading to many television appearances and talk shows, in addition to which she has also authored many books.

Linda Goodman is a name I would be remiss not to mention. As a teenager I read all her books from page to page, absorbing every single word and enjoying her wit and humoristic interpretations. With an array of books to her credit, as a New York Times bestselling American astrologer, and earning the distinction of being the first astrologer to do so, she made astrology fun for everyone, turning a boring old "science" into something that almost reads like a romantic novel. To her credit, metaphysical consciousness and the New Age movement came into focus through her writings.

Astrology is a fascinating subject leading to cosmology and energy. As the primordial energy that connects all human beings to the cosmos, being a higher power, astrology is an enigmatic canopy that can guide us through life by previewing events, forecasting, and advising us, so we have some knowledge of who we are, and pick up hints about what is in store for us. Ultimately it is our choice to follow along the path that is highlighted according to our planetary dignities and get ahead with the knowledge provided. We do have free will to make choices, however. On a well-lit path, we may tend to make better choices. Marriage compatibility, synastry, and other important indications gleaned from the horoscope can lead to well-informed and wise decisions. Since the onset of the coronavirus pandemic, there has been a renaissance of astrology, with an incredible surge of interest among the younger population.

To download free software to calculate your natal chart on the basis of sidereal astrology with moon placement, visit the website for Jagannath Hora.

HOROSCOPE

Our natal chart or horoscope is literally a picture of the sky at the exact time of our birth. All the planets, stars, constellations, asterisms, and pretty much every celestial body are kind of freeze-framed to form the birth chart, which acts as a blueprint of our lives. Surely most of you have indulged in excitedly checking out your daily horoscope in the newspaper or an online article or have skimmed through the magazines in the grocery store checkout line. This innate curiosity to know what lies ahead makes astrology so interesting. Listed below are some of the celestial bodies that directly affect our esoteric abilities and dreaming potential.

THE MOON

The moon, also called Luna, orbits planet Earth as its only satellite. The first day of the week is named after this rounded astronomical body, which lights up the night sky. Having other romantic names such as "Celene" and "Cynthia" or "Chandra," the moon generated enough interest for humans to explore it. In fact, the noun "moon" is derived from Proto-Indo-European "mensis," or month. Interestingly, "mensis" also refers to the female menstrual cycle, which occurs every twenty-eight days or so and is more commonly referred to as a "period." Astronautic expeditions to the moon have confirmed the presence of water on the surface. Composed of an external magnetic field, the moon is an exceptionally large body orbiting and influencing the earth, causing such things as tidal waves and eclipses.

From an astrological perspective, the moon is also the fastest-moving "planet," spending roughly two and a half days in each zodiac sign. The moon has affected humanity far enough for a lunar calendar to be calculated, versus a solar calendar.

The waxing and waning of the moon, as a dark, mysterious astronomical body lighting up the night sky, and the full and new moon cycles have long been purported to affect and influence human behavior and psychology. Even philosophers such as Aristotle believed in the connection between the water-filled human brain and its direct association with the lunar cycle. In current times also, it is popularly believed that during a full moon, people can go crazy or be driven to do insane acts.

Many esoteric and divination forms such as the Tarot regard the moon as having a very profound influence on the human psyche. There is evidence to be found in ancient stone carvings, tablets, and drawings in caves of the belief that our ancestors had in the power of the moon to influence dreams and intensify prophesying abilities. The shamans, witch doctors, and female priestesses believed that the lunar movements opened the door to sacred realms of mysticism and prophecy.

They relied on nature and lunar cycles and revered them as significant indicators of weather, nature, environmental occurrences, and ancient wisdom. According to Merriam-Webster, the word "mantic" is derived from the Greek word "*mantikos,*" meaning "prophet." "Mancy" is a relative of "mantic," with its distant relative being "mania." Additionally, the ancient Greeks believed that prophesying was a sort of madness. Mantis therefore is the art of divining and prophesying and the ability to engage with the energy of the moon for esoteric knowledge and inspiration.

In astrology, the moon is also associated with dreams, and the ability to explore the subconscious realms of the human mind. Key placements in the natal chart can indicate the ability and extent of the power of dreaming, astral travel, and the exploration of other realms. Anyone is capable of all these abilities, regardless of their planetary positions. But certain placements in the birth chart of an individual make these events more conducive and natural, and to a certain extent easy.

The placement of the moon in the eighth or twelfth house predisposes an individual to have prolific dreams. Sexual dreams, too, since the eighth house also deals with sex. Scorpio is the eighth house of the natural zodiac, ruled by Mars and Pluto. In Greek mythology, Pluto is the god of the underworld, the mystical gatekeeper. Pluto can be the most transformational; it encapsulates the subtle power of the unseen. Mysterious and secretive, the eighth house represents among other things the occult, the esoteric and metaphysical, and anything that is hidden below the surface, including death and dreams, astral travel and transformation, psychology, magic, and tantra. In fact it is truly a house of secrets. Like the twelfth house, the eight house is somewhat of an "underworld," which makes it the perfect place for dreams to thrive. Elusive and mysterious, a strong eighth house, or one with a stellium of planets, can induce powerful dreams for the subject.

In addition, there are nodes to the moon: the north node and the south node, which in Vedic astrology or Jyotish are referred to as Rahu and Ketu, respectively. Rahu or the north node is believed to influence more dreamlike, illusionary events, and Ketu, spirituality. The transit of Rahu over the natal moon in the birth chart can trigger altered states of consciousness, trancelike events, and dreams.

Since very ancient times, omens exerted an enormous influence on mankind. Dreaming about the moon itself is considered an immensely powerful omen. As the main significator of our soul, the moon acts as a luminary to reflect our inner-most thoughts and secrets. Dreaming of the moon therefore is an extremely significant occurrence, although rare. How the moon appears in the dream is how the omen translates. If the moon is bright, above the horizon, it bodes well as positive and auspicious and portends an advancement in life.

A waning moon or one below the horizon may not be a very auspicious omen. In fact, it can be considered as a warning of a not-so-fortunate event to arise.

Similarly, the size of the moon and its light and luster are factors that determine the nature of the omen. If the moon is clear and lustrous, it is a positive sign; if dark or blemished, not so positive. A thin crescent moon in a dream can indicate forth-coming good news or new beginnings. A disappearing moon in a dream could mean the lack of solidity to your plans. An eclipse in a dream represents transformation and change.

ASPECTS OF THE EIGHTH HOUSE

While calculating placements of planets in individual zodiac signs, it is imperative to respect the coordinating aspects as well. In Vedic astrology the moon and most planets have a one-to-seven aspect and a particular significance when occupying the actual house. If the moon is placed in the second house of the horoscope, it directly aspects the eighth house as well. Which means that it is almost tantamount to being in the eighth house. Or if the moon is placed in the sixth house of the natal chart, it will thus aspect the twelfth house, which also bodes well for having lavish dreams. Transiting moon in your eighth or twelfth house or having an aspect to both eighth and twelfth house also activates dreaming capacity. Besides, the full moon occurring in the eighth and twelfth houses, eclipses, and other lunar events all acerbate the dream state.

NEPTUNE

Neptune is that icy, cold, blue planet zillions of miles away from the earth, nebulous, foggy, and mysterious. Made of hydrogen, helium, and methane, it absorbs red light and reflects blue light, due to methane's gaseous composition. Interestingly, the planet Neptune was discovered by Johan Galle in 1846 on a prediction made by Joseph Le Verrier. Not only is Neptune icy and dense, but it is also the windiest planet. This outermost known planet in the solar system is known to have brightened significantly between 1980 and 2000. Named after the Roman god of the seas, associated with the Greek god Poseidon, Neptune therefore represents water and is also referred to as "the wild child." Neptune is the ruler of the ocean and life's deepest mysteries, as well as spirituality, intuition, dreams, psychic sensitivity, imagination, mysticism, the subconscious mind, and altered states of consciousness.

A strong placement of Neptune in the birth chart bodes well for achieving good sleep and dreams. If conjunct with another planet or luminary, such as the sun, the moon, Mercury, Mars, or Jupiter, it magnifies the ability of Neptune by strengthening it. An examination of the glyph of Neptune, which symbolizes the trident of Poseidon, shows the downward-facing cross, above which is placed a cuplike crescent, looking upward for direction and inspiration and possibly desiring to explore the unknown. As the ruler of Pisces, which again is a water sign, Neptune's hidden depths can be experienced just like the churning sea of Poseidon/Neptune. Providing colorful dreams and out-of-body experiences, a prominently placed Neptune can give many psychic gifts and spiritual advancement, and the ability of harnessing the energy of the universe to gain awareness and insight into its mysteries.

Also known as the higher octave of Venus, Neptune amplifies all kinds of illusions, fantasies, the psyche, and boundaries, boundaries that must be transcended when traveling from one realm to another and elevating consciousness. As "*the last planet*" in the solar system, Neptune rules the last or twelfth house of the zodiac, along with Jupiter. Pisces is naturally an intuitive sign, and a placement of Neptune in Pisces or an aspect to the sign of Pisces would intensify all the aforementioned attributes. According to Vedic astrology, Neptune placed in the first, third, fifth, eight, or twelfth house would also trigger significant psychic and dream experiences.

PLUTO

Discovered in 1930, Pluto is called the dwarf planet, one-third composed of water. Pluto however does play a very powerful role in influencing the zodiac signs. As the ruler of Scorpio, along with Mars, it corresponds to the Greek god Hades, the ruler of the underworld. Although slow moving, the energy of Pluto is intense and transformational. Just like the hidden nature of Scorpio, Pluto deals with spiritual growth and rebirth, subconscious forces, unseen elements, and energies of the unknown and hidden.

Interestingly, Neptune and Pluto spend many years in the same zodiacal sign. Pluto placed in the sign of Scorpio or the eighth house can generate a very intense nature toward death and its mysteries, the cycle of birth and rebirth, and reincarnation. In short, Pluto is the truth-seeking master of transformation. Pluto placed in Pisces can make the subject somewhat obsessed with the occult and dreams and interested in exploring the edge of the conscious world and inner growth. All in all, Pluto represents a very metaphysical planet, intensely connected with metamorphosis, transcendental beliefs, and a willingness to explore the deeper meaning.

THE TWELFTH HOUSE

Along with the importance of the planetary placement and aspects to the twelfth house, the ruler of the twelfth house is an important consideration. Whether the twelfth house falls in the sign of Pisces or any other zodiac sign, the signification stays the same. If the lord of the twelfth house in a birth chart is placed in the eighth or twelfth house or aspects of either of these two houses, it would surely have significant influence on dreams and altered states of consciousness. The twelfth house is the last house in the zodiac, the destination, the ending before the beginning, and the house of rest and collective consciousness.

Situated below the horizon, the twelfth house represents darkness, the unseen world, the completion of the cycle of life, letting go, and detachment. The twelfth house also stands for moksha, the final liberation from the karmic cycle of birth and death and the acknowledgment of the importance of spirituality. Referred to as the house of the unconscious, instinct, and dreams, it is in the twelfth house that we explore the deeper levels of the mind. In fact, the twelfth house can refer to the collective unconscious of all humanity, and things beyond the human plane.

Things such as astral travel, out-of-body experiences, near-death experiences, and other mystical experiences literally make this house a virtual dreamland. With a benefic spiritual planet such as Jupiter lording over this ultimate house in the zodiac, it points to positive transformations as a house of final review and rebirth. The moon situated in the twelfth house will enhance all aspects of these attributes. Neptune situated in the twelfth house will behave similarly. In the natal chart of Cheiro, an extraordinary occultist, the twelfth house is very strong with the placement of sun and Saturn. Jupiter which is the ruler of the twelfth house in the natural zodiac, has a tenth aspect making him a powerful seer. Interestingly, since the tenth house represents career and profession, Cheiro switched professions, earned tremendous fame, and made a lasting impression more as an astrologer, palmist, and numerologist.

NEPTUNE ASPECT

Neptune in the sixth house will aspect the twelfth house and trigger the imagination and psychic potential, provide vivid dreams, and elaborate otherworldly experiences. A moon placement in the sixth house will behave similarly, intensifying dreams and psychic experiences, visionary thoughts, and ideals. Abraham Lincoln, who was responsible for abolishing slavery in the United States, had his moon placed in the twelfth house, which explains his desire for reformation and the establishment of freedom from outmoded practices. Not only was he a great visionary and administrator, but he was also extremely psychic and intuitive.

The extraordinary account of Lincoln envisioning his own dead body in a coffin is ample proof of his psychic powers. Visionaries and creative artists of all types can find their inspiration with the fertile energy of the moon in the twelfth house. William Blake, the well-known author, poet, and artist, had his moon in the twelfth house, as did Paramahansa Yogananda, who was deeply spiritual and highly evolved. Paramahamsa Yogananda was an Indian yogi, mystic, and guru who was responsible for introducing the teachings of meditation and kriya yoga, was the founder of the Self-Realization Fellowship, and is the author of the book *Autobiography of a Yogi* (Yogananda 2015). Possessed of a strong intuition, he explored the far depths of existence, meditation, and yoga, samadhi and moksha, development of the soul, cosmic consciousness, and mysticism.

Neptune placed in Pisces, which is the natural twelfth house of the zodiac, brings a heightened awareness of all the attributes mentioned above. Cheiro, an occultist par excellence in the fields of astrology, numerology, and palmistry, had Neptune in Pisces in the asterism of Revati, which is noted for endowing psychic and metaphysical talents. This is a retrograded Neptune at that, which is much stronger. Cheiro was known to be highly psychic and metaphysical (refer to the natal chart for Cheiro on the right). A stellium of planets in the twelfth house is a significator of other worlds and realities, outer dimensional travel, mediumship, channeling, the occult, and of course dreams and dreaming. A transit of either moon or Neptune over the twelfth house will emphasize twelfth-house-related significations, although to a lesser degree. Jupiter, as the ruler of the natural twelfth house of the zodiac, wherever placed will subtly influence the twelfth house as well. Finally, the twelfth ruler of the twelfth house placed in his own house has the strongest signification; it behaves almost like an exalted planet, once again magnifying qualities and attributes of the twelfth house.

From a mythological perspective, the twelfth house is the home of Persephone's underworld, of which she is the queen, the goddess of death, and wife of Pluto. David Bowie, the super-talented rock star, had the sun and Mars conjunct the twelfth house with mercury on the cusp of the eleventh house, which is a sort of stellae. There are many world-famous personalities and successful people with prominent placements in the twelfth house, including the former US president Barack Obama. Nina Simone, an American singer, songwriter, and performer, had the moon in her twelfth house, and it is no wonder she could travel so far out to infuse so much soul into her music, which earned her the title "High Priestess of Soul." Nina was later inducted into the Rock and Roll Hall of Fame in 2018.

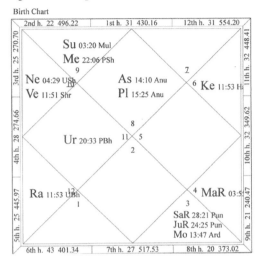

Birth Chart

Natal chart of Nostradamus with Sagittarius ascendant

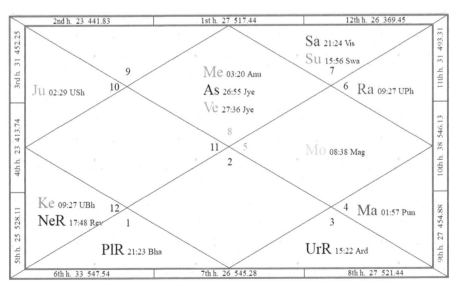

Natal chart of Cheiro with Sagittarius ascendant

Apart from the actual signs and houses, in Vedic astrology the importance of nakshatras cannot be discounted. The nakshatras, numbering twenty-seven and by some accounts twenty-eight, are lunar mansions occupying 13 degrees, 20 minutes of each zodiac sign. These constellations correspond to the astronomical stars such as Regulus and Aldebaran. Depicting many qualities and characteristics of the planets placed in them, these lunar mansions are an important study in the innate nature of man and his disposition. Each nakshatra is further divided into four parts called padas (steps or divisions), which provides a more detailed and defined explanation. The calculation of these celestial bodies begins with 0 degrees of Aries and ends on 30 degrees of Pisces. The fast-moving moon travels through each nakshatra in a day, wielding tremendous influence on these lunar mansions (also known as the twenty-seven wives of the moon). Since the moon is very strongly associated with our mind, imagination, dreams, and occultism, the placement of these nakshatras in the individual's natal chart can provide many clues to the nature of his mental thinking and talents.

As a matter of fact, the moon plays a primary role in ascertaining the notable events of an individual on the basis of its placement in the natal chart, which is also referred to as the moon chart. The nakshatra placed in the sign of the zodiac where the moon is present at the time of birth is known as "Janma Nakshatra," or birth star. The moon placement therefore is vital to judging the entire horoscope. Once again, this book will not cover extensive information; only relevant information connected to the subject of imagination and dreams will be covered here.

BHARANI

The nakshatra deity of this mansion, symbolized as the vagina, is Yama, the god of death, who is, like Hades, a guard of the underworld. Yama guides the soul to the astral plane. With Venus as its ruler, Bharani is in the zodiac sign of Aries, and ranges from 13 degrees, 20 minutes to 26 degrees, 40 minutes, corresponding to 35, 39, and 41 Arietis all together.

Holding the second place in the nakshatra list, the signification of Bharani is that of major change and transformation, such as entering the portal to another world, internal changes arising from a deep soul-searching experience, and contemplation of otherworldly phenomena. The female sexual organ represents the raw energy of creativity and the intense search to unearth the mysteries of life and death and the transportation of the soul from one body to the next. The boat as its alternate symbol stands for the transportation between different planes and realms of existence. In

Egyptian accounts, Anubis, the keeper of the underworld, guided the dead in his boat. Karl Marx had his moon placed in Bharani. Carl Jung had an extraordinarily strong Bharani position. Both these men searched deep in the womb for transformational and revolutionary ideas that they in turn sowed into the world as seeds or eggs.

ROHINI

The moon, which is exalted in Rohini, is also its lord. This makes for a highly imaginative, intuitive, artistic, and dreamy nature for an individual with a placement of such type. Supposed to be one of the brightest stars, the astronomical name is Aldebaran, and the Rohini nakshatra ranges from 10 degrees, 0 minutes to 23 degrees, 20 minutes in the sign of Taurus. The Hindu god Krishna is said to possess this placement, which bears testimony to his great powers of foresight and brilliant futuristic vision. Governed by the Hindu god Brahma, creator of the universe, Rohini symbolizes creation, fertility, conception, and growth. With so many attributes associated with the moon, the individual with this placement can achieve immense success by converting these talents into actions. As the fourth nakshatra of the zodiac, Rohini nakshatra aims for spiritual liberation or Moksha. Enhanced by Venus, the ruler of Taurus, Rohini nakshatra natives can expand their artistic and imaginative skills with beauty and receptivity. Some prominent personalities with this placement include Bob Dylan, Marilyn Monroe, and Sigmund Freud. Sigmund Freud is well known as one of the pioneers in the world of dream study.

MRIGASHIRA

Symbolizing the deer head, Mrigashira ranges from 23 degrees, 20 minutes in Taurus to 6 degrees, 40 minutes in Gemini, corresponding to the constellation of Orion. The ruling deity of this nakshatra is Soma, the god of immortality. Representing the seeker, natives of Mrigashira are on a constant hunt to fulfill their curiosity. As the fifth nakshatra, creativity rules those born under this asterism. Soma, as the ruling deity, drives these natives to investigate and explore the esoteric, spiritual, and unknown paths.

Inspired by the energy of the moon, Mrigashira natives have a great propensity to imagine, dream, and astral-travel. Forever seeking new knowledge, this nakshatra makes the individual more sensitive and perceptive, even psychic. The mystical nature of the Mrigashira natives can make them good guides and gurus, clairvoyants, and astrologers. By exploring the depth of life and finding answers to unexplained questions, they lead the path for others to follow.

ASHLESHA

Ashlesha, the ninth in order of the zodiac, ranges from 16 degrees, 40 minutes to 30 degrees, 0 minutes in Cancer. Known as Hydra or the clinging Naga (serpent), the ruling deities are the Nagas, who are deities of wisdom residing in Nagaloka (the underworld). The serpent qualities of astuteness, insight, and tenacity lend themselves to the native of this nakshatra, giving them a mystical ability to pierce through the core of any matter. Philosophical and spiritual, Ashlesha natives can make good astrologers and yoga instructors, enabling them to utilize their knowledge and powers of kundalini awakening and sadhana (spiritual practice). Past-life knowledge, ancestral information, and secret wisdom are other traits of this nakshatra. A notable personality with Ashlesha was the Buddha, who attained enlightenment at an incredibly early age after pondering the cause of suffering and sorrow.

JYESTHA

Ranging from 16 degrees, 40 minutes to 30 degrees, 0 minutes in Scorpio, Jyestha is the eighteenth in the zodiac. The ruling deity is Lord Indra, the king of Gods, and the symbol is the talisman, which stands for mysticism. Corresponding to Antares, Jyestha is also known as the eldest. Colored by scorpion attributes, natives of this nakshatra are intense and artistic and expand their imagination and dive deep toward new pursuits. With an interest in occult studies, astrology, and numerology, and coupled with their psychic abilities, these natives can secretly channel their talents toward philanthropic activities. They can also make good shamans or Aghoris (ascetic beings who seek freedom from the cycle of reincarnation). Scorpion tendencies of a watery, dreamy nature are hallmarks of Jyestha natives, pushing them to explore the supernatural and tantra.

PURVASHADA

The twentieth nakshatra, Purvashada ranges from 13 degrees, 20 minutes to 26 degrees, 40 minutes in Sagittarius, corresponding to Delta Sagittari. These natives are naturally philosophic and have a special liking toward spirituality and the occult, are ruled by Apas or the cosmic waters, and are deified by God. The essence of Apas or flowing water has considerable energy, which can be channeled spiritually by Purvashada natives. Associated with the legend of "The Ocean Churning," this nakshatra is enormously powerful, fluid, creative, and productive, leading natives with this asterism toward new paths and ideas. Also known as "the invincible star," these natives are highly imaginative and dreamy and spiritually inspired toward careers of psychic mediums and hypnotists. The Sagittarian qualities of courage, determination, and perseverance aid them in seeking spiritual meaning. As the initiate of the occult mystery schools, purvashada natives can make excellent spiritual teachers and gurus, motivational speakers, and counselors, even alchemists. Gifted with artistic skills, these natives can present metaphysical discoveries in an innovative way, in publishing, paintings, sculptures, or other media. A notable personality was Adolf Hitler, who was reputed to be a decent artist. Other prominent people include Ernest Hemingway, Rajneesh (Osho), and John Milton.

REVATI

The twenty-seventh nakshatra Revati ranges from 16 degrees, 40 minutes to 30 degrees, 0 minutes in the sign of Pisces and completes the series of Nakshatras. Corresponding to Zeta Piscium, Pushyan is the ruling deity who provides protection and nourishment to the animal world, as well as guidance and protection on one's path. Symbolized by the fish, Revati is naturally associated with the sea, enhancing attributes of a watery, dreamy Piscean nature. Endowed with tremendous imagination and intuition, the Revati native possesses the power to transcend and look beyond the ordinary. Fantasy and imagination rule the minds of these natives. Astrology and astronomy are natural interests for this psychic nakshatra, and they possess an extraordinary ability of clairaudience.

TELEPATHY AND DREAMS

At times you may think of someone randomly, and then you receive a phone call, email, text, or other form of communication from them. Or you randomly bump into them at the grocery store or post office during an unplanned errand. Simply put, that is telepathy. The transference of thought from one person to another, outside the normal human senses or physical interaction. This transference can also occur from a human to an animal or from one animal to another. Have you ever wondered how your pets communicate, how they sense your thoughts and emotions? The ancient Egyptians, who strongly believed in the power of dreams as messages from the divine, tried to communicate these messages with others in the dream state to pass them on.

There are many instances in the Islamic, Christian, and Judaic scriptures of telepathic influence in dreams. One of the more notable dreams of this kind is that of Nebuchadnezzar (Daniel 2:1–35), in which he awoke one morning to find that he could not remember what he felt was an oracular dream. After unsuccessful attempts by his dream interpreters to revive this memory, Daniel was consulted. Daniel was a Jewish youth in the court of Nebuchadnezzar who had the ability to interpret dreams, as mentioned in the book of Daniel. With the help of prayer, Nebuchadnezzar's dream was re-created in Daniel's experience and related to Nebuchadnezzar, who recognized it with delight as his own. Telepathic experiments are continually being conducted for scientific veracity; nevertheless, many prominent psychologists, including Jung, have validated its legitimacy. Unfortunately, fraudulent practitioners have given telepathy a bad rap. Along with clairvoyance and precognition, telepathy has been described as ESP (extrasensory perception) or psi.

The ancient Egyptians and Greeks were experts in transferring thoughts from one mind to another in dreams. In fact, as Cathleen Small states in *The Science of Mind Control and Telepathy,* "Mark Zuckerberg, the founder of Facebook, commented in 2015 that he believes the future of communication is in telepathy. He thinks technology will be the key to sending thoughts directly to other people. While it might sound like a distant dream, he may not be wrong" (p. 35). Telepathy can induce dreams that are far reaching and distant.

For instance, I can sometimes tap into the mind of my sister, who is 10,000 miles away, and have a dream of what she is cooking at that very minute. We compare notes the next day, and it works like magic. There is a ten-hour time difference between our geographical locations. When I am sleeping, she is cooking lunch. The way this works is that I first state my dream, and then she reveals what she has prepared, which confirms what appeared in my dream. This is so much fun that I urge you to give it a try. As with everything in life, practice makes perfect. At first you may not connect, but trust me, in time you will. Practicing telepathic skills not only improves your dream quotient but also strengthens your psychic muscle for other things, such as psychometry (reading the energy from objects like photos), mediumship (connecting with spirits), and precognition. You will be able to pick and choose what you wish to do, which in turn amplifies your ability to dream and astral-travel.

Dr. Stanley Krippner has conducted several research experiments regarding dream telepathy, which have been life transforming. "Our main surmise is that the psyche of man possesses a latent ESP capacity that is most likely to be deployed during sleep, in the dreaming phase. Psi is no longer the exclusive gift of rare human beings known as 'psychic sensitives,' but is a normal part of human existence, capable of being experienced by nearly everyone under the right conditions. . . .We may discover ourselves to be less alienated from each other, more capable of psychic unity, and more capable of closeness in ways never suspected. . .Perhaps all forms of life are vitally interrelated in ways we do not yet clearly understand" (Ullman et al. 1973, p. 227).

Therefore, with regular practice, anyone can dream telepathically for personal enrichment, for entertainment, and to develop intuitive faculties. You can even participate in the dream telepathy contests held each year by the International Association for the Study of Dreams (IASD). Telepathic dreams can manifest in numerous ways. Communicating with someone either on the phone or other media is the most common manner we can experience telepathy in dreams, as we do in waking lives. Astral travel and out-of-body experiences also trigger telepathy when ideas are communicated without an actual conversation taking place.

We spend an inordinate amount of time checking our email and text messages, which would naturally carry over into our dream sphere. Sometimes, the actual voice of a person can be heard in a dream. Although rare, this can be a direct read of that person's thought, almost like a hands-free text message reader. In this example a friend of mine had a dream in which a particular gentleman confessed that he was in love with her. Finding this rather strange, since he also happened to be her co-worker, she decided to make a joke out of it. One day at lunch, she nonchalantly announced to her group of coworkers that she had a very silly dream in which "Mr. Y" professed his love for her. Imagine her surprise when one of the ladies exclaimed that she was aware of this fact, since "Mr. Y" had confided in her. Thoughts have wings. Strong emotions and associated thoughts have the power to travel like a messenger to communicate silently and sometimes more effectively.

PALMISTRY AND DREAMING

One of my fondest memories as a child of seven years was when my dad, a talented palmist, remarked, upon observing my palm, that I had an extraordinary line of head. In fact, I have two lines of head. I didn't quite grasp the meaning of the word "extraordinary," and my dad in his best way equated it to "long" for a child's comprehension. At that moment, I started to develop an interest in palmistry and began voraciously reading my dad's vast collection of books on the subject. By the age of eleven I was reading the palms of family and friends. Whenever I saw a lengthy line in someone's palm, I would inform them that they had an extraordinary line. Of course, they were overly impressed, thinking they had some special ability, but that didn't last long since I eventually caught up to the meaning of the word "extraordinary."

Like astrology, or any of the ancient forms of divination, palmistry has been around for an exceptionally long time. There are various schools of palmistry and several variations of palmistry, those with origins in India and those practiced widely in other parts of Asia, Sumeria, and Babylon. From India, the knowledge of palmistry traveled to Greece and other parts of Europe, where Anaxagoras is believed to have practiced it. Anaxagoras was a Greek philosopher who propounded the theory of *Nous* or cosmic mind. A treatise about palmistry is said to have been discovered by Aristotle, who in turn gave it to Alexander the Great, who was very much intrigued with it. But the Catholic church was opposed to any kind of divination, including palmistry, and actively discouraged it, which may have led to its disuse in the Western world.

In modern times, the most prolific figure in the field of palmistry was Count Louis Hamon, who studied palmistry in India for two years and started a professional practice upon returning to the UK under the pseudonym Cheiro (derived from chiromancy). Also known as chiromancy, palmistry in the time of Cheiro was still a controversial subject, not having gained any kind of authenticity yet. Cheiro, with his magnetic personality and undeniable charm, was successfully able to attract many notable and famous personalities of his day. His practice flourished as his reputation spread far and wide across the world as an exceptionally reliable palmist making accurate predictions not only about people but even about world events. The list of clients who lined up to visit him included celebrities such as Mark Twain, King Edward VII, Oscar Wilde, Mata Hari, and several top socialites. The czar of Russia and the notorious Rasputin, who was given a detailed reading regarding his death, were included in this vast list of famous clients.

Palmistry is an extensive subject involving the study of the shape of the hand, shape of the fingers, shape of the nails, the lines in the hand, and other features. The intention of the inclusion of palmistry here is to briefly enumerate the connection of the ability to have dreams to the hand. There are seven types of hands, each of which can be further subdivided. The study of the shape of the hand is called cheirognomy.

TYPES OF HANDS

The Elementary Hand

The Spatulate Hand

The Square Hand

The Conic Hand

The Philosophic Hand

The Psychic Hand

The Mixed Hand

Some hands are obvious to discern and easily fall into one of the descriptions previously mentioned. In my experience of decades of palm reading, I have observed that most hands have a somewhat mixed appearance, and there could be a blend of some types, which may be a little challenging to spot. However, there will be a dominant characteristic of one of the basic types that must be taken into consideration, as well as some contiguity in the lines of the hand that will validate the primary shape of the hand. The shape of the hand, furthermore, may be different from the shape of the fingers. For instance, one may have a square hand with psychic fingers (I did tell you this is a complex science).

The Elementary Hand

Some books on palmistry state that the fingers should always be longer than the palm to distinguish this type of hand. This is not always the case, especially in the elementary hand. The palm is heavy, thick, and quite coarse, while the fingers may be short, equal to the size of the palm, or very short. This kind of a hand indicates a love for basic needs, very elementary as the name goes.

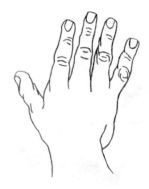

Elementary Hand

The Spatulate Hand

With an exaggerated wrist, the spatula here refers to the tool the chemists use in a mortar. The base of the wrist is significantly wider than the rest of the hand, gradually pointing toward the fingers, which could be long and curvy, like they are holding on to a small object. From my observation, this type of hand is one of the easiest to identify. Sometimes it can be overly broad at the base of the fingers as well. If the hand you examine triggers an image of a spatula, rest assured that it is so. This is the hand of the inventor and the creator. This person likes to dig for information. They could also be archeologists. Explorers and discoverers also can be identified with this shape.

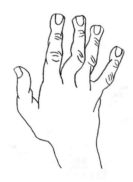

Spatulate hand

The Square Hand

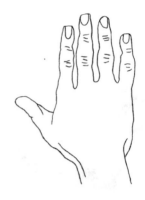

This hand is characterized by a square wrist and square fingers; the nails are short and square as the rest of the hand, which denotes extreme practicality in many areas, such as work, career, practical sciences, and subjects that are oriented more with reasoning rather than instinct. The square hand with short, square fingers denotes a materialistic tendency, businesslike and practical. The square hand with long, square fingers is logical as well as practical. They are a little more open minded than the short

Square hand

finger type, but very bound by tradition, rules, and the customary path. The square hand with knotty fingers, which are usually long as well, indicates a meticulous person. This person takes pride in producing a perfect piece of work, whether it be related to art, science, or medicine. The square hand with spatulate fingers is still on the same track of practicality, logic, and method, but these people are inventors of useful, practical items such as household tools and equipment.

The square hand with conic fingers takes a detour from the rest. Conic fingers represent imagination and intuition; this hand could be that of a musical composer. Artistic, yet solid and methodical, the artistic nature of this hand will translate to material success, more so than the purely conic or psychic hand, which may not necessarily translate to worldly success. The square hand with psychic fingers is quite unusual, almost like an oxymoron exhibit. Like opposites together, this type will be scattered in their thoughts and projects, lacking solidity to their plans. Imagination may exist, but the direction of it may not prove fruitful. The square hand with mixed fingers is quite common and is seen mostly in men, not women. The fingers will be of all mixed shapes, pointed, spatulate, square, not concurring to any one type. Staying within the basic parameters of logic and reasoning is characteristic of the basic square hand, and the assorted fingers lend versatility and inspiration that is blended with the purely practical.

The Conic Hand

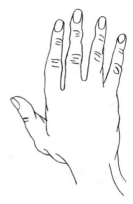

Conic hand

Also known as the artistic hand, it can sometimes be confused with the psychic hand. Here the palm is less narrow, with fingers that are full at the base and have slightly pointed nails. This hand denotes an artistic, impulsive nature, although a little impatient. These people are fond of luxury and are easily influenced. Being somewhat impulsive, they possess quick thinking but rarely put their thoughts into motion. As well as being quick tempered, they are prone to speaking their mind without placing any filters. Artistic attractions such as color and music appeal to their senses and emotions, which could evoke extreme reactions such as joy and sorrow, and elation and despair. Generous to the core, they are certainly interesting and make good conversationalists. Public life appeals to owners of the conic hand, and the shape of the fingers indicates the direction they may take for their platform. The spatulate fingers can lend more originality and courage, while the square fingers may lend more endurance.

The Philosophic Hand

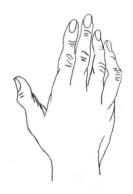

Philosophic Hand

One of the easier types to detect, the philosophic hand is long and angular, with very thin bony fingers, with obvious joints and nails. This type of personality is very deep and philosophic, the thinker. Whatever they engage in, they infuse it with mysticism. More interested in the deeper mysteries of life, they like to explore beyond the normal boundaries, seeking knowledge and secrets. Subjects such as ancient mysteries, history of religions, secret practices, and such are some things they are attracted to. Many yogis and mystics are found with this type of hand. Dreams, visions, tantra, yantra, out-of-body experiences, and the exploration of other realms are the highly revered pursuits of the philosophic type.

The Psychic Hand

This is an incredibly beautiful hand in appearance, a very pure, soulful one invoking the qualities of Psyche, the Greek goddess of beauty and soul. Just as Psyche was subject to the jealousy of Aphrodite and came under her command and influence, the owner of the psychic hand may also have some hardship to contend with. The psychic hand is characterized by long fingers, almond-shaped nails, a narrow slender palm, and a very delicate

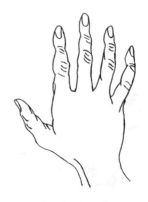

Psychic Hand

appearance overall. Inherent with the psychic hand are visionary, idealistic, dreamy, imaginative, and highly intuitive capacities. People with a psychic hand are attracted to all kinds of magic and mystery. Being of a sensitive nature, they make the best mediums, psychics, and clairvoyants. Dreams and the dreamworld with all its avenues are the playground of this type of hand.

The Mixed Hand

The mixed hand is exactly that, nothing significant that one can label or classify as any one of the other six types. Somewhat rare, in a class of its own, the mixed hand is very versatile and can have fingers that are also mixed, not belonging to any one type. If a hand does not fit exactly into any one of the other six types, chances are it is a mixed hand. Extremely adaptable, this type can go anywhere the wind blows, changing course, professions, homes, or anything that is necessary

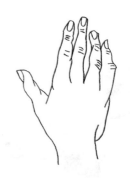

Mixed Hand

or desired. This mercurial quality can lend itself to developing an interest in the esoteric, dreams, and the paranormal world, whether briefly or otherwise.

THE NAILS

Nails are generally classified into four types: long, short, broad, or narrow. Long nails indicate an artistic, imaginary type, with a good aptitude for esoteric and artistic subjects. In my practice, I have noticed that people with broad nails that are more rounded or moon shaped are deeply sensitive to the tidal fluctuations of the moon. Eclipses and such events trigger dreams and imaginative powers in these individuals.

They seem to be greatly affected by lunar activities.

THE MOUNTS

At the base of every finger on the palm side of the hand, lies a little pad that may be somewhat raised or not, called the mount. At the base of the thumb lies the mount of Venus. The mount of Jupiter is at the base of the first or index finger. The mount of Saturn is situated at the base of the second finger, the mount of sun can be found at the base of the ring finger, and the mount of Mercury at the base of the fourth finger. In addition to these mounts is the mount of Mars which is located in between the mounts of Venus and Jupiter. Also called the higher

Mounts on the Hand

mount of Mars due to its placement, if well developed it would indicate a fighter, someone who is highly independent and sometimes too impulsive. Between the mounts of Mercury and the moon lies the lower mount of Mars. If this is highly developed, it could indicate an interest in occultism and secret societies. These individuals make natural hypnotists and mentalists. A well-developed mount of Mercury would indicate writing and communication skills. The mount of moon or Luna lies exactly opposite the mount of Venus. This mount is highly significant as it is related to the moon and if well developed can indicate elevated levels of imagination, visions, dreams, and a search for deeper meaning and profound experiences.

CHIROMANCY

The study of lines on the hand as well as different shapes and formations is known as chiromancy. The intention of this book is to focus only on aspects related to the power of dreaming, intuition, and related esoteric concepts. Therefore, relevant applications will be described, with a brief list of the major lines of the hand.

THE LINE OF LIFE

Circling the mount of Venus, underneath the thumb, is the line of life. It commences under the mount of Jupiter and slopes down toward the mount of Venus. The line of life is mostly indicative of the subject's health, vitality, and longevity.

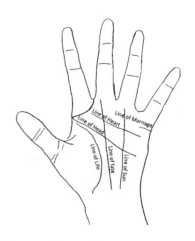

Principal lines of the hand, depicting the major line

THE LINE OF HEAD

The line of head is generally observed next to the line of life and can arise from the center of the mount of Jupiter, from the mount of Mars, or from the line of life itself. Characteristics represented by this line include talents, ambitions, aspirations, and mental temperament, as well as others. The line of head with an exaggerated slope denotes great imagination, artistic skill, metaphysical interests, and pursuits. Likewise, a line of head leaning toward the mount of Luna or sending an offshoot to the mount of Luna highlights interest in mysticism, exploration of the esoteric, occult, dreams, and astral travel. A double line of head, although rare, with one line veering toward the mount of Luna, also indicates vivid imagination and heightened metaphysical abilities. In relation to the philosophic hand, if the line of head is set high and travels straight, the subject will be fearless to pursue anything of interest, be it mysticism, out-of-body experiences, or the like. In relation to the conic hand, when the line of head is straight, the subject will be more practical with his artistic and imaginative talents. Using intuition to guide the imagination, this person will successfully implement their esoteric ideas in a worldly way. In case of the psychic hand, which is naturally very dreamy and visionary, the line of head naturally slopes. If the line is unusually straight, it indicates that the subject has gone through some transformation and become more practical.

THE LINE OF FATE

Also called the line of destiny, the line of fate is found in the center of the palm, rising upward and commencing from the line of life, the actual wrist, the mount of Luna, the line of head, or the line of heart. This line is usually a little hard to detect, being amid all other lines that may crisscross the palm. This line denotes career, success in worldly accomplishments, influences from others, fortunes, riches, social position, and power, as well as misfortunes, difficulties, and hardships, on the basis of its placement.

THE LINE OF SUN

The line of sun can arise from the line of life, the mount of Luna, the mount of Mars, the line of life, or the line of heart. The key in analyzing this line is to connect it with the type of hand it represents. Dealing with success, fame, and renown in life, this line is also referred to as the line of Apollo. If the line of head is sloping, and the line of sun arises from the mount of Luna, it indicates success in ventures of an artistic, imaginative, esoteric nature. There exists the potential to explore the metaphysical and supernatural, along with the possibility of success and fame in the same field.

THE LINE OF HEALTH

Rising from the base of the mount of Mercury, the line of health travels down, toward the line of life, and is sometimes faint or absent altogether. Also called the line of hepatica, it indicates ill health, disease, and death. Therefore, an absence of this line is a positive sign, leaning toward robust health.

THE LINE OF INTUITION

This line is shaped like a semicircle from the mount of Mercury to the mount of Luna. As the name indicates, the line of intuition indicates extraordinary powers of imagination, dreams, intuition, mediumship, clairvoyance, and other esoteric abilities. When this line is found in the psychic, conic, or philosophic hand, these attributes are heightened. As extremely sensitive beings, individuals with this placement can make good healers and therapists, such as Ayurvedic and Reiki practitioners and acupuncturists.

THE GIRDLE OF VENUS

Extremely rare to be found, this line arises in between the base of the first and second fingers and ends between the third and fourth fingers. Denoting an extremely sensitive nature, individuals with this placement can be high-strung and nervous and possess a tendency toward depression.

THE LINE OF MARRIAGE

One of the more interesting lines, the line of marriage can be found on the mount of Mercury at the base of the little finger. Generally concerning relationships as well as marriage and divorce, the line of marriage indicates obstacles, happiness in marriage, or unhappiness and divorce.

Beside these principal lines and their formations, there are shapes such as the cross, star, circle, island, chain, grill, island, and others than can be found on the palm. Once again, only relevant descriptions will be enumerated, as significations of imagination and the subconscious. The star is a fortunate sign in most placements keeping the shape of the hand in mind.

STAR ON THE MOUNT OF LUNA

By now you may have guessed the importance of the mount of Luna with respect to the subconscious realm. A star formation on the mount of Luna therefore will enhance dreamy, imaginative qualities that can lead to even greater success and fame. This could manifest as a career as an author of spiritual and esoteric work, or even as a psychic medium performing for large audiences, holding gallery-style performances, conducting seminars, webinars, podcasts, and workshops.

THE CROSS

Contrary to the star, the cross is not a fortunate sign on any type of hand except when found on the mount of Jupiter, where the cross indicates the possibility of a positive romantic relationship. If a cross is situated on the mount of Luna under the line of head, it could lead to an excessive imagination with a fatalistic tendency.

THE SQUARE

One of the rarer signs, the square acts like your "lifeline," something that protects and shelters you through a storm or disaster. The square can enable one to avoid disasters and crisis. On the mount of Luna, the square can protect the individual from the negative influences of exaggerated imagination and esoterism, and an overindulgence of the same, like a psychic overkill.

THE ISLAND

The island is generally not considered a fortunate sign; however, the negative effects of the island are restricted to the area of the hand it is located in. On the mount of moon, the island indicates a challenge in developing imagination and intuition. This type of positioning would generally also indicate a poorly developed mount of moon.

THE CIRCLE

Only when found on the mount of sun is the circle considered fortunate. On any other mount, the circle indicates a negative influence. If the circle is attached to any of the lines on the hand, the individual will be traveling in circles, confused and dazed to free himself of the situation or problem. If the circle is found on the mount of Luna, there could be a danger of drowning.

THE GRILL

Wherever the grill formation is seen on the hand, it denotes misfortune in the area it represents. For instance, on the mount of moon, the grill would mean a tendency toward a restless and overly anxious disposition, even melancholic tendencies.

THE TRIANGLE

The triangle is a distinct formation to be found on the hand, not to be confused with the mere crossing of the lines on the hand. When it appears on the mount of Saturn, the triangle indicates an expertise in psychology, intuition, and mysticism. An attraction to the occult and metaphysical studies and hobbies all are indications of this position. On the mount of moon, the triangle formation lends itself to a more scientific aspect of the imagination, occult studies, and its development. Therefore, the triangle is a sign of success in whatever area it is placed, on the basis of its signification. Sometimes the triangle may be mistaken for the diamond, which is a different shape with its own meaning. For purposes of brevity, we will exclude some of the shapes of lesser significance to this study.

LA CROIX MYSTIQUE: THE MYSTIC CROSS

Like its name suggests, the mystic cross is a special formation not to be confused with the regular cross. In fact, the shape does not resemble a cross, but rather an oblong or diamond shape. This formation can be found in between lines, especially between the line of head and the line

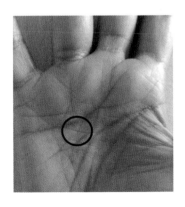

Mystic cross: one of the symbols in the hand denoting a psychic ability

of heart, although in a rare case the mystic cross may appear as an individual formation by itself. Usually placed in the upper center of the hand, the mystic cross is **the** signification of all things mystical; hence its name. With this placement, the subject can even be a seer or a prophet, able to foresee events precisely. All things unknown, unseen, and mysterious are the hallmark talents of this placement, indicative of possessing a prominent level of arcane wisdom. A true visionary, the subject with this formation can be an expert in several methods of divination, such as astrology, palmistry, mediumship, dreams, visions, and a host of other modalities. With a desire to help others with their visionary talent, the owner of the hand with the mystic cross formation can also make a successful career and achieve worldwide fame and success, especially so when it touches the line of fate.

THE RING OF SOLOMON

Situated below the mount of Saturn, the ring of Solomon or Saturn circles the entire mount of Saturn, forming a semicircle in between the index and ring fingers. This formation also indicates an elevated level of expertise in occultism, the metaphysical, dream and imaginative powers, and the ability to time-travel lucidly through past lifetimes. In the diagram the mystic cross and the ring of Solomon are present in the same hand, which exaggerates the mystic powers.

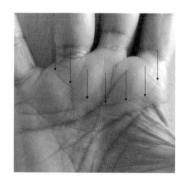

Solomon's ring: a rare formation found in the hand

CHAKRAS AND DREAMS

Chakra is a Sanskrit word meaning a wheel or vortex. The chakras are energy points in our body that correspond to our emotional, spiritual, and psychological health and well-being. There are more than one hundred chakras, but the main ones, which number seven, are the principal points of focus. With the insurgence of yoga and meditation today, the chakras have become a crucial tool as force centers for spiritual enlightenment. Originating in India, the chakras are now widely used by psychics and mediums to connect with spirits and delineate the cause of death of discarnate souls in a reading. Development of certain chakras can strengthen powers of the imagination, dreams, and astral travel, as well as promote good health by releasing blockages, blockages that cause health ailments and issues when these chakras are

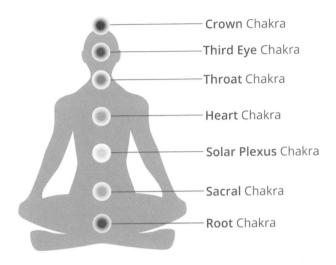

The seven main chakras

not in alignment with the nerves, organs, and other areas connected with them.

Detailed information on chakras can be found in the Vedas, ancient sacred texts of India. Chakras, also known as disks, are described as petals of a lotus flower, vibrating with assorted colors and intensity according to the physical and emotional health of the human body. Beginning from the base of the spine and traveling to the crown of the head, each of these chakras is assigned individual names, associated with stones, tones, elements, and properties aside from colors. The elements are to be recognized more as states of matter rather than the actual chemical elements themselves. More importantly, chakras hold your *prana* or life force. Chakras also store an abundance of personal information and knowledge, memories, thoughts, and experiences. People with advanced clairvoyant faculties can sense the chakras. This body of subtle information in turn affects our behavior and actions externally. Knowledge about chakras makes us conscious of the diverse levels of extraordinary awareness.

There are several ways to connect with these chakras and work to keep them aligned and direct the flow of energy to vibrate positively. Modalities such as Reiki, meditation, visualization, acupuncture, crystal healing, sound healing, chakra balancing, hypnotherapy, and yoga, to name a few, which have gained immense popularity in recent times, are a means to connecting with the chakras. A timely connection made with the chakras can aid in rebalancing and redirecting the flow of energy to fix any issues that are needed.

With regular work, chakras can be cleansed, activated, and energized as blazing, rotating whirlpools of a lotus. These chakras vary in size, brightness, and development from one person to another. Chakras can be balanced and strengthened in numerous ways, such as meditation, mantras, and crystal work. An advanced chakra such as the crown chakra can appear brilliantly hued, almost like a golden halo that extends to the etheric body, which is extended by just about an inch or so from the physical body. The following is a list of the seven main chakras, with a special emphasis on those individually associated with imagination, intuition, dreaming, and other esoteric practices.

MULADHARA, ALSO CALLED THE ROOT CHAKRA

Also called the root chakra, since it is located at the bottom of the spine near the tailbone, muladhara represents your root force and materiality. This root chakra connects you to the earth and grounds you with a sense of extreme practicality and earthiness. This chakra also connects you with the necessities in life and helps you with survival modes, grounding, and

The mudra for the root chakra

pro-tection. The name muladhara is derived from the Sanskrit word "*mula*," which means root or foundations, and therefore this chakra helps you stay connected to the earth. Represented by red, the shape of this chakra is a square or a yantra, surrounded by four lotus petals. Within the yantra lies a triangle with a linga, around which a snake is coiled three and half times. Herein lies your source of power, where the first beginnings of manifestation, such as abundance, take place. Naturally, the symbol of the muladhara is the earth, the associated sound or mantra is "*lam*," and the stones associated are the black obsidian and the red garnet.

SWADISTHANA, ALSO CALLED THE SACRAL CHAKRA

The second chakra, called swadisthana, is located at the sacral center, roughly an inch or so below the navel. Associated with sexuality and creativity, this chakra is symbolized as the crescent moon, surrounded by six lotus petals. Orange, the element of water, and the mantra "*vam*" are other associations of this chakra. Orange is a very bright, cheerful, and friendly color, and the combination of red and yellow denotes a highly social nature, and an ability to radiate. For esoteric development, this chakra is a kind of warehouse of subconscious memories, past-life memories, and other hidden information. Instinct or gut reactions arise from this chakra, as the crescent moon lends its dreamy, imaginative powers to stimulate intuition. In addition, the swadisthana chakra regulates the urinary tract, the reproductive system, and the testes for men. For women, this chakra is particularly important since the uterus and ovaries are located here. The endocrine system can also be regulated by balancing this sacral chakra. The stones associated with this chakra are the tiger's eye and carnelian.

The mudra for the sacral chakra

MANIPURA, ALSO CALLED THE SOLAR PLEXUS CHAKRA

Symbolized by a downward-pointing triangle, surrounded by ten lotus petals, manipura is associated with fire and the color yellow and regulates digestion and metabolism. Located at the solar plexus area of the body, this is said to represent the conscious mind, ego, and creativity. When this chakra is in balance, you feel comfortable in your own skin, even empowered and motivated, literally "fired up" with Agni or the fire element radiating like a jewel. Development of this chakra is vital for astral travel, out-of-body projections, and interdimensional travel. This chakra is reflective of the energy of the sun, being bright, yellow, luminous, and cheerful. The mantra for this chakra is "*ram*," and the stones associated are citrine, turquoise, and malachite.

The mudra for the solar plexus chakra

ANAHATHA, ALSO CALLED THE HEART CHAKRA

The fourth chakra, anahatha, also known as the undefeated, is located at the heart. Unconditional love, compassion, empathy, kindness, forgiveness, bliss, harmony, purity, and other humanitarian qualities are associated with this chakra. The symbol of two trangles, one pointing upward and the other downward, with twelve petals on the outside, is the shape of this chakra. Corresponding to the element of air and the color green, when the ana-hatha chakra is balanced and pointed upward, the positive qualities are enhanced. Green is also the color of nature, healing, and herbs, which have curative, nurturing properties. Green jade and rose quartz are some of the stones associated with the anahatha chakra. The mantra for this chakra is "*yam.*"

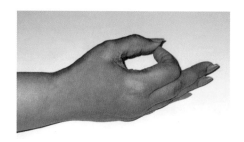

The mudra for the heart chakra

VISHUDDHA, ALSO CALLED THE THROAT CHAKRA

Located at the throat, vishuddha is the fifth chakra, representing the element of ether and shaped like a downward-facing triangle with a circle within and surrounded by twenty lotus petals on the outside of the triangle. The blue color of this chakra stands for communication with others and self-expression. Regulating the thyroid gland and metabolism, vishuddha is also called the throat chakra. Blue has a cool, calming, soothing effect, and when the vishuddha chakra is well balanced, emotions, authentic expression, and harmonious communications are also centered and balanced. The mantra for this chakra is "*ham,*" and the corresponding stones are sodalite and azurite.

The mudra for the throat chakra

AJNA, ALSO CALLED THE THIRD EYE CHAKRA

One of the more well-known chakras, the ajna chakra, also called the third eye, is located in between the eyebrows. The Sanskrit meaning of ajna is "beyond wisdom"; thus it corresponds to spiritual awareness, intuition, clairvoyance, telepathy, accessing other dimensions for divine messages, lucid dreaming, astral travel, and other metaphysical abilities. Signifying the subconscious mind, the ajna chakra represents all five elements of ether, air, water, fire, and earth, since it transcends through space. The pineal gland is associated with the ajna chakra, which is shaped like a circle with a small downward-pointing triangle enclosed within, surrounded by two lotus petals on the sides of the circle. The relevance of the location between the two eyes is the synchronization of the left and right sides of the brain.

The supercenter of consciousness and psychic power is focused in the third-eye chakra, where spiritual access is infinite. As the seat of the deepest wisdom, higher intuition, telepathy, astral travel, and past lives, other esoteric modalities can be explored and understood. Representing the pineal gland, the ajna chakra is the seat of the memory

The mudra for the third eye chakra

archives and is stimulated when the kundalini is awakened. Spiritual and higher vibrations, transcendence into higher realms of consciousness, imagination, dreaming, clarity of thought, inner vision, ESP, creative visualization, achieving trance states, and feeling bliss are other attributes of the ajna chakra. As its Sanskrit name suggests, the ajna chakra is truly the portal to perception and awareness. The symbol of this chakra is a downward-facing triangle enclosing a yoni to represent the dual powers of Shiva and Shakti. A circle flanked by two lotus petals surrounds the triangle, the color is indigo, the element is telepathy, and the mantra is the all-encompassing "*om.*"

Lapis lazuli is the stone associated with the ajna chakra. Favorite of the Egyptians, lapis is an exceptionally powerful stone with dizzying powers. The jewelry of the ancient Egyptians served more than just the purpose of providing visual beauty. The Egyptians believed that the power of the lapis stone could protect, guide, and connect them with the spirit guides and was an important addition to their burial treasure. The powdered lapis was popularly used for the manufacture of makeup. In fact, the tomb of King Tutankhamen was richly laid with lapis lazuli. The ancient Hebrews wore garments embedded with lapis lazuli, and the ancient Greeks and Romans used them extensively for decoration. The Sumerians believed that lapis lazuli encapsulated the spirit of the deities and helped form a relationship with spirit guides. The Persians were extremely fond of this mesmerizing stone. Considering its tremendous power, one must proceed with caution while using this stone. Besides aiding in psychic endeavors, the lapis lazuli has health and healing properties.

Especially important for having dreams and invoking spirit guides, lapis lazuli enhances astral travel and spiritual journeys. Apart from its healing properties, lapis lazuli also protects the individual against psychic attacks. Considered a lucky stone from the time of the Renaissance, lapis lazuli is highly prized even today as the wisdom stone, representing the mystical world. Lapis lazuli can be used to unblock the ajna chakra, to gain more clarity and vision, and to invoke and enhance the dream experience and access the Akashic records. You can meditate holding the lapis lazuli or by placing it nearby.

SAHASRARA, ALSO CALLED THE CROWN CHAKRA

Known as the thousand-petaled lotus, the sahasrara chakra is the portal to the heavens. Sahasrara in Sanskrit means "infinite," and therefore this chakra is symbolized as the infinite source of wisdom and spirituality, containing memories that store information. Located at the very top of the head, sahasrara is commonly referred to as the crown chakra. At this center, the lotus is completely bloomed, unfolding consciousness.

The mudra for the crown chakra

Containing all colors, this chakra radiates brilliantly, reflecting a gold halo around the head. This primary chakra is the final of the seven chakras, regulating brain functions such as memory, cognition, and intelligence. When the sahasrara chakra is activated, positive energy flows, bringing spiritual understanding and enlightenment. This is the final journey of the kundalini merging of Shiva and Shakti, the yin and yang. A feeling of oneness and superconsciousness is achieved with perfect balance. Divine energy is united with the guru within, creating a blissful state of higher power and meaning. Dissolving ego consciousness, the soul feels ecstatic and free, reaching toward Samadhi or enlightenment.

Symbolizing the color violet and the mantra "*om*," the sahasrara chakra has no element, just pure divine consciousness. The sahasrara chakra regulates both the pituitary and the pineal glands. Attached to this chakra is the silver cord that links the astral body to the physical body. This cord is utilized for astral projections and out-of-body experiences. There are accounts of people who have observed the silver cord during their astral travel and near-death experiences. Upon death, this cord is severed, separating the physical body from the astral body. Therefore, the silver cord acts as a protective shield to guard the physical body from venturing too far into the cosmos and by keeping the physical body grounded. During an intense journey of astral projection, it is possible to observe the silver cord.

Associated with this powerful crown chakra is the beautiful stone of amethyst. A darling of psychics and metaphysical practitioners, the amethyst promotes healing and bestows protective powers from negative energies. The Romans dedicated this stunning stone to Neptune, the water god. Herein lies an important psychic parallel to the astrological sphere, as aforementioned in the astrology section, where the planet Neptune is associated with dreaming. Known for stimulating the third-eye chakra as well, the amethyst has been known to activate the imagination and the power of dreaming and prevent intoxication of any kind. In earlier times, it is said that the Romans added an amethyst stone to their wine cup, and Christian priests wore rings made of amethyst.

KUNDALINI AWAKENING

Kundalini is a divine feminine energy that lies dormant at the base of the spine. Representing Shakti, depicted as a snake coiled three and a half times around the spine, and resembling the medical symbol the caduceus (the staff of the Greek god Hermes), the staff represents the spine. With intense meditation and yogic practice, this kundalini energy can be activated to reach greater heights of spirituality. There are other methods to awaken the kundalini energy, and one of them is by dreaming. When this occurs, it is an extremely powerful experience, a highly transformative event, and a primal force of awakening of a mental, emotional, and spiritual nature. This energy travels through all seven chakras along the spine and culminates in the crown chakra, where higher consciousness is stored. Unlocking this power can lead to bliss, and the spirit of oneness. Intuitive powers, ESP, dreams, clairvoyance, astral travel, out-of-body experiences, past-life regression, mystical experiences, empathic abilities, and compassion are other attributes that may be experienced with a kundalini awakening along with an extraordinary sense of inner peace and joy.

There is a transcendence of spirit, a change in consciousness, increased spiritual connection, and awareness of your body that can also lead to better health, well-being, and a long-term positive change. All these powers can transform your life, reduce stress and anxiety, and improve cognitive function and creative powers. As an aid in astral travel, kundalini energy fearlessly facilitates the easy transfer of the etheric body into the cosmos. The presence of kundalini even intrigued the curiosity of Carl G. Jung. Jung explored the kundalini experience with respect to the unconscious, making a connection with the consciousness and unconsciousness through the process of individuation.

Letting go of ego is vital to the awakening of this powerful energy, and the effects of the awakening can sometimes be challenging. The process is unique for everyone, since everyone has a unique experience; they may even have a different type of transformation. The physical manifestations of the kundalini are many and varied. It is imperative that one desiring this kind of transformation is fully prepared to handle the process effectively. Also called "*Shaktipat*," kundalini awakening can be activated by near-death experiences, when the ego is temporarily distended and the vast realm of consciousness is pervaded with a brief encounter with the other side, as the veils between the two worlds thin, and cosmic awareness takes the shape of a higher vibrational journey of divine intelligence.

Mandala: a beautiful design with a lotus motif in the center
(courtesy of Kamlesh Rajesham)

MANDALAS

Nowadays, mandala art has become a popular as well as a colorful hobby. Everywhere you go, in stores and online, there are innumerable coloring books and other art projects. The word "*mandala*" is Sanskrit for circle. Very much like its twin of sorts, the chakra, the mandala is a circle with many dimensions. Yogis and meditators often contemplate on the mandala, which encloses within it a square with a deity in it. The roundness of the mandala represents wholeness, and its purpose is to gain inner knowledge that can lead to profound insights and transformation. At the very center of the mandala is an eye. In a way, the eye that you focus on, is looking back at you. In the Indian, Tibetan, and Japanese cultures, the symbol of the mandala is very sacred, forming a symbolic relationship with the cosmos and the self. Shiva, the Hindu god of creation, is depicted in a circle as Nataraja, signifying the endless cycle of birth and death, the loop of infinity of creation, unity, and harmony. The concept of sacred geometry is also present in the structure of the mandala, as a means of drawing the focus in and leaving the physical world out. By narrowing and directing the vision to the center, the mandala becomes an image of sharp focus.

"The Mandala is an archetypal image whose occurrence is attested throughout the ages. It signifies the wholeness of the self," states C. G. Jung. Jung was the first to introduce the concept of mandalas to the West, employing the mandala to gain knowledge of the potential and complexities of the self. Jung echoed some of the same beliefs expressed in the ancient Vedic texts of India known as the Rig Veda to elaborate on his theory of "Collective Unconscious." Jung included the mandala in his list of archetypes, as representing transformation and an established order, and as "an instrument of contemplation" Jung explains, "The energy of the central point is manifested in the almost irresistible compulsion and urge to become what one is, just as every organism is driven to assume the form that is characteristic of its nature, no matter what the circumstances. This center is not felt or thought of as the ego but, if one may express it, as the self." In "Archetypes," Jung further states, "The mandala represents the monad and corresponds to the cosmic nature of the psyche. . . " (Jung 1973)

Rich in symbolism, the mandalas also represent the petals of a lotus, which is again tied to the chakra symbolism. There is an interconnectedness between the external image of the mandala and the chakras within the human body. The lotus is one flower that transcends the murky waters, blossoming into a beautiful flower with symmetrical petals. The square within the circle represents the four directions of the compass: north, south, east, and west, representing completeness and the essence of the universe. There are several types of mandalas, making them extremely versatile for serving different purposes. For instance, a dream catcher has a mandala theme for the purpose of protecting the individual while sleeping and to ward off evil spirits. Sand mandalas are a prominent art form for many Native American tribes, such as the Navajo Indians, who regard it as a symbol of the impermanence of life. They use the shape of the mandala as the medicine wheel to heal a sick person and nurse him back to health. They also believe in the power of the mandala to bring inner peace and harmony spiritually as well as emotionally. The Indigenous shamans living in nature employ the mandala-shaped drum to enhance trance states to connect with the spirit world. Even the rattles, another tool of the shamans, have a prominent mandala-shaped head atop the stick.

The healing power of the mandala has been documented widely. Used in therapy, mandala art and diagrams are becoming enormously popular in hospitals and medical institutions in recovery and healing programs. The very act of creating a mandala has beneficial therapeutic effects. Regarded as the best expression of the self, mandala art can explore the very core of your inner being and release repressed emotions and traumatic memories. The mandala can represent the inner self and therefore heal by its very expression, release stress, and encourage deep reflection. Jung himself created several mandalas, which totally changed his way of thinking. In his own words, "I sketched every morning in a notebook a small circular drawing, a mandala, which seemed to correspond to my inner situation at the time. With the help of these drawings, I could observe my psychic transformations from day to day. . . . Only gradually did I discover what the Mandala really is: 'Formation, Transformation, Eternal Mind's eternal recreation.'" (Jung 1972).

The Notre Dame Cathedral in Paris, France.
Take a note of the circular formations.

Mandala motifs appear in numerous art and architecture examples throughout the world. The beautiful church of Notre Dame in Paris, France, has two mandalas on its exterior wall, with a spectacular stained-glass mandala display on the interior walls of the church. The mandala motif is an architectural element frequently seen on church exteriors throughout the world. The geometric configuration of shapes and symbols within the mandala is representative of the self, embracing both masculine and feminine energies, making it complete, as the energy of Shiva and Shakti. The shape of the mandala, however it may vary, draws your attention to the center, to focus and meditate. The mandala inspired Jung to a great extent. He relates his experience and explains his system thus: "I had to abandon the idea of the superordinate position of the ego. . . . I had to let myself be carried along by the current, without a notion of where it would lead me. When I began drawing the mandalas, however, I saw that everything, all the paths I had been following, all the steps I had taken, were leading back to a single point—namely, to the mid-point. It became increasingly plain to me that the mandala is the center. It is the exponent of all paths. It is the path to the center, to individuation." (Jung 1957).

In other religions and cultures, we find the mandala concept employed in prayer and worship and in spiritual and devotional practice. The Tibetan version of the mandala is more traditional. Tibetan monks regard the mandala as a sacred image that can be created through the power of imagination only by the instruction of a lama. These types of mandalas are unlike the popular images we see frequently today. The Islamic mosque in Mecca, considered the holiest shrine for Muslims, has a square-shaped construction in the center of an enormous courtyard. The square structure called *kaaba* (cube) is covered in silk, where worshipers dressed in white circumambulate it in a choreographed fashion while chanting, resembling a perfect mandala of human movement.

Pennsylvania Dutch hex sign on a building in Lancaster, Pennsylvania.
A close-up of a traditional red barn with a hex sign in Pennsylvania.

The Pennsylvania Dutch have hex signs all over their farms and homes. These hex signs are circular and colorful and represent birds and flowers as protectors of their farm animals and pets. The different signs and symbols are used to ward off evil and function as harbingers of good luck, fortune, and happiness. Some of the hex signs are more complex, resembling a traditional mandala with geometric patterns inside. Thought of as folk art, these hex signs are a sacred tribute to the stars and heavenly bodies, representing the mysterious and supernatural. Referred to as *schtanne* (stars), these decorations are popular spiritual traditions that can be found even today. The four points in the hex sign are like the four directions of the traditional mandala. These large and bold hex signs can be seen on barns and buildings from a distance, adding color and beauty to outdoor structures. Other points and features of the hex signs are associated with Christian beliefs and traditions, as well as astrology.

A type of mandala called the Shri Yantra is an ancient mystical symbol. This is more geometrically formed with nine interlocking triangles that come to a point called a Bindu. These triangles radiate outside toward the cosmos while representing the human body. Shri means wealth and refers to Laxmi, the goddess of wealth. Yantra means a machine or instrument. Out of these nine triangles, four of them point upward, representing the ultimate universe, and five of them point downward, representing the regular world. Once again, like the traditional mandala, there are four doors that open to the four directions: north, south, east, and west. The lotus is also a significant part of the Shri Yantra since it is also the deity contained within. The Shri Yantra can be as complex a formation as desired. Basically, as a means of worship, devotion, focus, concentration, and spiritual advancement, the Shri Yantra can quickly induce a meditative state. The designs can be created on various materials, such as paper, sand, rice, flower petals, and others, and its uses extend to vastu (Indian feng shui) to attract positive vibrations to the living space, office, or elsewhere.

The Shri Yantra is a magnetically powerful image to induce a higher level of consciousness and a means to create your own reality. Clearing negative energies and removing obstacles, the Shri Yantra can be utilized to transcend beyond your limitations and fears; it facilitates you to harness the pure cosmic energy and positive vibrations to attain peace and harmony, and spiritual and material abundance. The effective method practiced with the Shri Yantra is this: By focusing on the center, the dot or Bindu, you expand your vision to the small triangle that encloses the Bindu, then gaze on the opposing triangle. The upward-facing triangle represents male power, and the downward-facing triangle, divine feminine power. Shift your focus next to the circles; they represent infinity, a loop that has no beginning or end. The lotus leaves represent grace, understanding, and openness. Lift your heart as you gaze deeply in the circles, feeling an expansion in your heart center and opening your heart to accept the creative energies unfolding. Slowly gaze at the square shape with its four portals of direction pointing to the material world, expressing the transition from the external world to the sacred internal space within the soul. While holding your gaze in this fashion, return your focus to the center or the Bindu. Feel yourself connecting within, then expand your focus slowly to include the whole image of the Shri Yantra, thus interlocking the internal and external aspects. This process is like a kaleidoscope, almost like a holographic pattern of expanding your gaze slowly outward and then back to the center. After you complete this, you can close your eyes. You may still see the imprint of the Shri Yantra reflected. Penetrating in this fashion, the energy of the Shri Yantra is crystallized.

5

Common and Uncommon Dreams

WATER DREAMS

Water dreams are rather common. Our bodies are composed mostly of water, we spend our early life in a womb of water, and, more importantly, we need water to survive! Apart from which, not only do we drink and cook with water, for hygienic purposes we also cleanse ourselves with water. Water therefore constitutes a significant and indispensable part of our daily existence, which is why water can have innumerable meanings. Likewise, in a dream, water also has various meanings: the direct or literal meaning, the symbolic meaning, and the spiritual connotation all have to do with how the water appears in your dreams. Whether the water is clear, muddy, flowing, stagnant, icy, or fountain-like, all the many details must be observed carefully and considered to derive the meaning. In a general sense, water can signify the emotional state.

For a few weeks in a row, I kept dreaming of water repeatedly. Mention was made earlier of the importance of recurring dreams. If you have the same object, in this case, water, appearing constantly in your dreams for a regular period, it could be a clue that it might manifest in your life in some way. While journaling this dream, I remember thinking how amusing it was to have all these water dreams and no possibility of cruising in these COVID-19 days, since water dreams sometimes indicate cruises for me. With no ship to board, what did this mean? Well, Hurricane Isaias hit Florida, and a couple of days later it arrived in my town, the effects being a torrential, nonstop, thirty-hour downpour with gusty winds, resulting in tree damage, power loss, and flooding. Despite a tornado warning being issued, I decided to go for a ride in my car on some errand. Almost arriving at my destination, which was less than a mile away, I came across a huge body of water, which covered the street from end to end. Just like in my dreams! By then, I was already committed;

there was no turning back. My car navigated that little but big pond and stalled just after, in the parking lot of a diner. Whew. I made it! Just then I heard sirens, as fire trucks, emergency vehicles, and even the news truck pulled up beside me. They promptly blocked the street I had just crossed as they continued their preparations. Wondering what to do, I tried to start the car, but only steam would come out. After about fifteen minutes, I tried starting the car again and it started. But I could not go far, since the car stalled on the side of a steep hill. Then I called a well-known car service for a ride, but there was no response. They probably had no drivers available. As I sat in the car, looking at the hillside and watching trucks precariously go by, I decided to pray. I started chanting my favorite mantras with all my heart. More than thirty minutes later, I tried starting the car again and it started! Wow! I continued driving home, keeping my eye on the odometer, counting the miles till I reached home. What an adventure! All I can say is that I was so glad that my water dreams manifested in a happy ending.

DROWNING

Dreams of drowning, whether in a swimming pool or river or sea, are common. Going underwater and coming right up with no struggle could mean a temporary glitch in some area of your life; you may have lost hope temporarily. If the drowning seems more nightmarish in nature, where you feel yourself in a panic, gasping for air, it could indicate something a little more worrisome with the issue you are facing. You may be feeling overwhelmed or suffocated with someone or something in your waking life or experiencing deep emotions and anxieties. You may find it difficult to handle something that seems overpowering. Particularly in an office environment, it may indicate a strong negative force at play. If in the dream it is you who is trying to drown someone, you may be trying to repress them or make them disappear. In case you happen to be witness to someone drowning, or if you can rescue them, it means you will have the opportunity to "save" someone or something. If, on the contrary, you are unable to save a drowning victim, it means your hands are tied regarding some situation in your life, making you feel somewhat powerless.

LATE FOR SCHOOL

In the second of a series of dreams, I was going to a class at a university. Upon entering the parking lot of the campus, two other cars were blocking my path, which delayed my entrance to the classroom, and the class was already in progress. To top it off, my registration information that I had sent ahead was also missing. After class, I asked the instructor for directions to the office. Meanwhile, a young girl, who was also late but got through her registration, offered to help me. She first asked me if I knew the instructor personally, and when I said no, she went on to explain that the registrar was the instructor's own father, and that he just made the registration process sound more important than it really was. She also offered to show me the place, after she was done getting a snack at the outdoor cafeteria. I went along with her, and she sat on the barstool eating. As I waited for her, I heard the name of the university: "Fairleigh Dickinson," which is an actual school in the state of New Jersey. The morning after, not knowing what to make of the words in the dream, I looked up the meaning of the words "Fairleigh Dickinson," since I have no association with it whatsoever, never attended it, and never knew anyone who did or anyone who had a connection with it, although it is a well-known private school. There was nothing about it in the news, and neither was I involved in any personal conversation about it. However, the fact that I heard it in my dream had to have some significance. Looking up the meaning, I found that in Latin it means "gently, strongly." In this case I needed the dictionary to translate the basic language, since there was no other way to interpret the sound.

This dream is common to have and typically indicates anxiety or expectation of some upcoming event in your life. Being late for school, missing class altogether, and finding an empty classroom or a wrong location, all have to do with the feelings of nervousness and anxiety about something. In relation to me, this dream did correspond to my thoughts and expectations of a project I was working on. Fairly simple, but there is another layer to this dream. The clue "Fairleigh Dickinson" was given to me as the answer that was underneath the basic meaning. Remember I heard it in my dream. Then the young girl offered to help me. When you apply these clues, it explains the process I needed to follow regarding the project, which was "gently, strongly," which in this case was guidance. This made so much sense to me, and I immediately took it into consideration and altered my approach. Everything is important in a dream, literally every little thing. At first it may seem so inconsequential, but upon further thought that little thing produces great meaning.

EATING

Another common dream reflecting an important activity in daily life is eating. We eat basically to satisfy hunger; we nourish our body and fuel it to provide energy for the day as well. In a dream, eating suggests hunger or appetite, and a desire or longing for some vital and necessary part of life such as love, comfort, and happiness.

If you are enjoying eating in a dream, it means you are enjoying life. What you eat is also important in deciphering the meaning. Meat can add a sense of heaviness to the subject: bread or rice as a staple food can mean home comfort, love, and basic needs. Chocolate in a dream suggests a luxury or a search for excitement, pursuing something hard to get. Biting into a donut is about coming "full circle" or a sweet ending. At times, food in dreams appears when you are on a diet and your subconscious reminds you that you are being deprived. Especially in the case of sugary items. Eating fruits in a dream can bring good news or lead to happy developments. A shared meal can indicate friendship, camaraderie, and good times. Very often, before a cruise I dream of eating in large groups of people. Some of the ships I have been on include upward of five thousand passengers! A dream in which you are dining outdoors can mean an openness of feelings and emotions, a sense of comfort with others, and being able to express yourself. Eating alone could mean the opposite: feeling lonely or isolated and friendless. Our relationship with food is a very crucial part of our life, body image, and expression. As mentioned before, it is extremely important to view the entire context of the dream.

FLYING

Flying in a dream has many connotations. Here the feelings and emotions felt during flying are the key to discovering the meaning. Many people have a fear of flying, and therefore a dream of flying could turn out to be a nightmare, riddled with fear and anxiety coming to the forefront. Feeling exhilarated while flying in a dream could be a lucid dream or astral travel. During lucid dreaming I often take my body off the ground and fly to escape something I do not like. Flying in a lucid dream is one way of changing the outcome of the dream. During astral travel, my flying has a purpose, a planned destination. In general, positive feelings about flying in a dream suggest a sense of freedom, liberation, and well-being, feeling powerful and happy. Conversely, fear-filled dreams of flying could mean a sense of feeling lost and out of control, a lack of confidence, or feeling ungrounded and imbalanced. Flying can take on a spiritual flavor since our perception of heaven is above. In this sense it could mean rising higher spiritually and connecting with your higher self. Often in lucid dreams I find myself flying higher and higher to experience something deeper.

FIGHTING

We have all had dreams of battling demons and dragons or being the superhero and fighting to release someone from the grip of evil beings. More common in children than adults, dreams of fighting are nevertheless a frequent event. During the day, we are engaged in the hustle and bustle of snagging that cab or elevator, grabbing that seat on the train or subway, and other activities where we are essentially "fighting." Not to mention the office squabbles or other petty quarrels and road rage incidents. This behavior is replayed to us in dreams, where we are venting and expressing anger, frustration, and resentment that had been suppressed earlier. Whom you are fighting with becomes significant. If it is an actual person or people that you know, consider your feelings toward them: Are you antagonistic, in some way misunderstanding them, or checking to see if there is any other issue that is blocking your path? If there are animals or other creatures you are fighting with in the dream, this could reflect your own thoughts and ideas. Reflect on what you are resisting in life or wrestling with, in your own mind.

DREAMS OF AN EX-PARTNER

Nine out of ten queries I receive are about dreaming of an ex-boyfriend or ex-girlfriend. This does not necessarily mean you will get back together or that you must get back together with each other, or that this could lead to a rekindling of the relationship. There are a few reasons for this kind of dream. Either you are replaying an old relationship, reliving it to find some clues or patterns that can help you in your current relationship, or are just being nostalgic about it. You could be revisiting the past to tie up loose ends and find closure to move on. Or some part of the old relationship has triggered a sense of fear and anxiety in your current relationship. If it were a good relationship that ended on a positive note, you could be missing some enjoyable element of that relationship. You may have qualms about your current relationship or about your own self. Relationships generally mirror your own self, and this is one way your psyche is revealing itself to you. Perhaps you are giving too much of yourself, or not enough; this is for you to analyze. You could still be hanging on to that ex and not fully engaged in your current relationship. However, it is not likely that your ex is pining for you, since this dream is more about you and your emotions. If that relationship was toxic, your subconscious is trying to help you by reminding you of past behaviors that need to be avoided. Trauma has a way of sticking around in your memory, to keep reminding you of what needs to be avoided.

RUNNING OR JUMPING

Unless you are a marathon runner and this is your profession, running in dreams implies escaping. Figuratively "running away from something or someone." For people who run every day as part of their daily regimen, it could just be an activity like everyday work. We shirk from unpleasant things in daily life, not wanting to face reality. A dream in which you see yourself running is the picturized version of this. Perhaps a new job or relationship is not up to your expectations, leaving you disappointed and unhappy. Running can also represent challenges and the necessity to deal with them. Running up and down hills indicates new opportunities and goals that need fortitude. Jumping in a dream also has several interpretations. If you are jumping in one spot, even repeatedly, it means you are in a sticky situation you may be trying to escape but cannot, feeling trapped and powerless.

Jumping long distance indicates reaching for higher goals and aspirations, like reaching for the moon. If your jump lands you on your feet without falling off, it reflects success, good fortune, making headway, successful endeavors, and positive news. Jumping over an object and landing on your feet indicates overcoming obstacles and hurdles, having courage and grit. Falling off after a jump could mean a failure about something in your life, making bad decisions or getting negative results. In general, if jumping appears frequently in your dreams, it describes your ambitious nature, and your determination to tackle new projects and ventures.

MONEY

Dreaming of money is all about your own self-worth and value, how you perceive yourself. It indicates your emotional state and resourcefulness, your value of and even your views about money. Finding money in a dream is a sign of wealth and prosperity, your positive sense of self, and power. You are driven to succeed, to follow opportunities and convert them to gains.

FIRE

Fire is a powerful energy, a necessity in our daily lives, and essential for life. How the fire appears in the dream will point out its positive or negative aspect. Some of the positive aspects are optimism, drive, passion, purification, innovative ideas, and creative beginnings. The negative aspects are extreme anger, temper, volatile behavior, and explosion. As a transformative symbol, fire can also signify the release of pent-up anger and emotions.

FOREST

Forest, trees, and woods in a dream are beautiful symbols of spirituality. Forest represents green, symbolizing life, fertility, harvest, and growth. Unless the forest appears dark and menacing, it is usually a good indicator of wealth and growth, abundance and prosperity. This abundance could manifest spiritually or materially and promises potential. If you are lost in a forest, it could mean that some situation in your life is unclear and dense, or there is an element of uncertainty as to which path to follow.

PARKED CAR

A dream in which your parked car is not to be found or you go searching in the parking lot to find your car suggests you have lost your direction or motivation. It can also mean that you have misplaced your drive in some inappropriate channel. If you are walking around the parking lot in circles to locate your car, it reflects your personal goals and ambitions. The car represents how you move in life, your direction. Your drive to move forward has been misplaced, misguided, or hidden. This directionless aspect may point to an element of uncertainty as to the direction in your waking life. Perhaps you are in the wrong field or job or geographical location. You may be lacking the satisfaction or feeling deprived of the benefits of something you are focused on, or it could mean that a lack of clarity brings self-doubt and hesitation. Another meaning could indicate that a specific aspect of your life seems to be hidden or out of view.

Taking an exit in a dream can indicate that it is time to leave a situation. Exit signs in dreams are highly meaningful. Often in life we are faced with making the decision of whether to stay or go, just as the song goes: "Should I stay or should I go?" We are reluctant to make changes, we resist change, and sometimes we continue with a situation even if it is not a good one, because of fear. When you see a stop sign on the highway, or you are taking the exit, consider this as a sign from the universe and make the necessary decision. A green light, on the other hand, can indicate that a path is clearing, that you are getting permission in some aspect of your life. Progress of some kind is likely.

TOILET

Dreaming of going to the bathroom, looking for a bathroom, or not finding one has to do with unexpressed negative emotions. Repressed feelings of frustration manifest in dreams of trying to get rid of, or getting rid of, waste or that which no longer serves you. Feeling an urge when your bladder is full, you seek to relieve it; similarly, in a dream, seeking a toilet signifies the need to find some relief with uncomfortable emotions or feelings. In a dream where you find a clogged toilet, or an incomplete toilet, or something that restricts you from getting rid of your "waste," it indicates a need for privacy or feeling unable to release your emotions. Such dreams are quite common among my actor friends. As public figures, the need for privacy becomes a basic need, as is the need to eliminate body waste. A clogged toilet is a sign of blocked or pent-up emotions and stresses, and a search for psychological relief. The act of eliminating in the presence of one or more people points to how you perceive the opinions of others, what people think about you in private. A neat and clean bathroom can indicate better things to come, a brighter outcome. A toilet without doors or separations could mean eliminating boundaries and barriers between people or situations. Standing in a long line for a toilet is something common in public areas such as malls, airports, and train stations. This event in a dream alludes to patience and perseverance, such as the act of literally counting the people ahead before it is your turn.

Toilet dreams can sometimes be gross and unpleasant; nevertheless, they deserve attention. Bottled-up stress and emotions must be released either through self-therapy or professional therapy. These dreams point to the necessity of releasing that anger or frustration and finding emotional peace. Examine recent events and relationships to find the cause and cure, or these dreams will recur. Find the source and take small steps toward resolution.

SNAKES

Another common dream element of many people during the COVID-19 pandemic has been snakes. Snakes generally represent growth, renewal, rebirth, and transformation. The snake sheds its skin and progresses, and its presence in a dream could signal positive movement. During the COVID-19 pandemic, a large number of people were involved with moving their homes, either to another city or state. Whether these people moved in to settle with parents and other relatives or moved out to smaller towns and farming communities, there was a transformation in their lives. Snakes could also represent health and healing. The kundalini energy that is awakened is coiled at the base of the spine and moves such as a serpent by techniques like meditation and other spiritual practices. The caduceus, an ancient symbol of medicine that is still in use today, has two entwined snakes around a staff. The necessity of finding a cure for the pandemic, coupled with anxieties of finding health resources, had many of us engaged in long, detailed conversations about health and healing.

UNCOMMON DREAMS: CHARMING MAN OR DEVIL INCARNATE

I had a dream the night before last, that there was a handsome, silver-tongued man who would woo women and kiss them, but he had a stinger at the end of his tongue (I think they then fell under his control or something). Anyway, I met this man and fell for his charm, but when I was stung, something else happened. It was more like a video game action where I would die, and in my next life I would meet him again in the same spot, but I remembered and with each life I ran from him, trying various things to get away or hide . . . weird.

This dream was sent to me for interpretation by a friend who could not figure out the meaning. I immediately asked her if she was fighting any bad habits or mild addictions. She was stunned because that described her exact condition. Admittedly, she was trying to curb her excessive desire for eating potatoes. How did I decode this dream? If you examine the narration line by line, you will notice a theme of temptation, a sort of devil pursuing women. In this case, the subject herself. Desperately trying to run away and hide describes her mental state of attempting to control her food consumption. The sting she mentions points to her realization that her health would be adversely affected.

ANUBIS

Another dream query I received was a dream of Anubis. In Greek mythology Anubis was a multitasking, half beast and half human, with the head of a jackal and the body of a man, black in color. His appearance in a dream has several interpretations. The name "Anubis" is the Greek version of Anpu, which meant "to decay," forming an association with death. The Greeks equated him with the god Hermes. He was the gatekeeper of the underworld, who judged souls by a feather on a scale alongside the heart of the dead soul. A lighter feather passed on to heaven, and a heavier one was devoured by the beasts. Anubis also presided over elaborate burial rituals of mummification and other preparations such as embalming of the dead on their journey to the afterlife. He was also the protector of graves, fulfilling many tasks. Anubis in a dream could mean protector, spirit guide, messenger, judge, caretaker, companion, ancestor, guardian, having to face a trial of some sort, or even self-judgment. In an esoteric sense, the jackal can aid in guiding us to access past lives. For Egyptians, the color black represents rebirth and fertility as a signification of the river Nile. Examine your emotions and find what fits the appropriate meaning.

ACT OF KILLING

In the year 2021 this had been a regular dream theme of many of my clients. In a dream they see a family member killing either them or the other way around with a sword, knife, gun, or other implement. Rarely does this imply the actual act of killing, murder, or dying. Rather it would imply killing a part of someone or something. Literally ending something that is uncomfortable or distasteful. The coronavirus pandemic and the lockdown are largely responsible for creating the circumstances causing these dreams. We dislike any kind of change in our routine and schedule called life. Yet, the pandemic forced us to make several changes to cope with drastic conditions of separation, loneliness, isolation, and sickness all at once, not to mention having to face the sudden death of family and friends. The tremendous pressure of making the necessary changes is the cause of these dream scenarios, inducing the helpless feeling of being lost and directionless, having to sacrifice and adjust, trying desperately to regain power and control of life. And ultimately accepting, however fearfully, that the end of something is inevitable. Identifying people in the dream and what they mean to you can provide further clues based on your relationship with them. If it is an ex-partner in the dream killing you, it could mean making peace and adjusting to the new reality of moving on and finding closure.

YOGA MANDALA

In this dream, I was arrested by the police, along with other people, since you could carry only $40 in your wallet at a time, and the rest of it had to be labeled. Next, we were all shepherded to a place where there were twenty yoga mats laid out on the floor. They were all blue in color. Someone pointed to a silver mat next to the wall and said that it was assigned to me. This was almost like a precognitive dream, since I was later cast to play an inmate on the Netflix series *Orange Is the New Black*. In the episode I was in fact shepherded by a police officer, along with other women, into an exercise room of the prison. We had overspent our allowance at the commissary and were being punished. All the other convicts were wearing khaki, and I was the only one made to wear white (which could symbolize the silver mat in the dream). Then, Constance Shulman, who plays the role of Yoga Jones, was lecturing to all the inmates about the benefits of mandala and chaturanga! I have to say that this was one of the longest scenes I participated in that season. All the clues in the dream lead directly to the meaning, which requires no explanation.

SEXUAL DREAMS

Erotic dreams, also called wet dreams, are triggered by emotions, feelings, and reactions that cause blood-pounding, heightened physical sensations, which can be very pleasurable and satisfying. Sometimes they can be more graphic and real than in waking life. The sexual organs in the body are aroused during this process, and climax can also be achieved. Sex in dreams can feel so real that some dreamers pursue these experiences in lucid dreaming. At times, the sexual movie in the dream can be strictly about the sexual union and nothing else. This can be one way the body satisfies its urges that were repressed during the day. During the day, sexual thoughts arise frequently in a normal person. External aids and stimuli such as films, magazines, novels, and other erotic imagery can trigger and stimulate the mind. A simple act of a kiss in a dream may indicate more of a want of appreciation than a full physical union, or even the need for more kindness and affection. Alternately, being kissed by someone unthinkable in waking life could represent an important aspect of that person, or an unrecognized quality or trait in yourself, such as creativity that has not been expressed or the development of a new idea.

Dreaming of sex with an ex-partner is a common query I receive from clients. Such dreams can be repetitive. This is more about letting go of the old relationship, and the issues or misunderstandings, rather than a desire to rekindle that relationship. This involves the act of closure to find healing. A particular frustration with a current relationship may cause stress and disturbance that bring memories of past relationships in this manner, as a way of sorting out the issue. With time, as the healing takes place, the recurrence of this type of dream slowly fades. Depending on the context of the dream, sex with an ex-partner in a dream could also suggest dissatisfaction with the current partner. Sometimes, working out these feelings with the help of therapy and changing your thoughts could cause these dreams to change.

A celebrity-involved sexual dream could be pure wish fulfillment. Daytime fantasies and desires could result in nighttime fulfillment. Movie stars, rock stars, or other celebrities are often portrayed as sexy, desirable beings, which exerts a large influence on the mind. Infatuation, crushes, and imaginary forays with celebrities and other publicized personalities cause an indelible impression on the mind that plays out in dreams. However, this is not always the case. Sometimes, it is not the desire to have sex with celebrities, but may have to do with the admiration of some other quality that the dreamer holds and would like to inculcate in their own self. The melding of this admirable quality can be symbolized by the sexual union, of embracing and incorporating some of these qualities into your own personality, to achieve success or fame. Some sexual dreams can directly point to one's own innate needs, desires, and longings.

Looking for a location to have sex is more about the need for privacy or intimacy. Perhaps your partner is overdemanding or needy, and you need some space. A sexual experience without achieving climax can indicate inherent frustrations, disappointment, and lack of fulfillment regarding some event in your life, or a person causing some frustration. If the dream involves making love in a public place, this can indicate an exceedingly elevated level of confidence and body image. You may wish to embrace public life, have a desire for the limelight, or want to be in the spotlight. Successful dieters who have achieved their goal of physical transformation can often dream of "showing off" in public in this manner. If, on the other hand, a sexual experience causes you embarrassment and shame, some aspect of your public life needs to be addressed. Or it could be that the partner in your dream is your conspirator in creating this state of embarrassment. If your parent interrupts your sexual interlude, this reflects their values and approval. If your sexual partner is not your spouse and you happen to be enjoying the experience, it could be a warning of parental disapproval. If your parents are witnessing your sexual act, feelings of guilt are festering in your mind. Parents represent teachers and archetypes of values.

SCARY DREAMS

Who likes them? Just as we like a sweet dream to be never-ending, we more strongly wish for a scary dream to end ASAP. Nightmares, dreams of death and dying, murder, divorce, illness, natural calamities, and disasters, however, are a part of life. In fact, they are inevitable parts of life. When we see unpleasant things in dreams, we tend to ignore them. I am myself guilty of this. But I have learned through time that I will have to face this eventually, and therefore I no longer ignore the preview that is being shown. In fact, I even feel obligated to inform the recipient who appears in the dream if it concerns them. Dealing with this kind of scenario is like the act of ripping that Band-Aid off. You can never underestimate the information and details given to you. This could potentially help in the avoidance of a car accident or a disaster from taking place in real life. When you have prior knowledge, you act accordingly and take measures to protect yourself. Or warn others of impending danger.

I had a dream where I was told that a young man I know was going to get divorced. In the dream, it was his uncle in real life (living) who gave me this information. Immediately I informed the young man, who was quite unhappy to hear this. He had been married a few months and seemed to be happy. In fact, he was about to purchase a home and secure a mortgage for it. But I advised him to postpone his plans just a little. What happened next took us all by surprise. Not even a week had gone by, and one day this young man came home from work to find the apartment empty! Only his clothes were left behind. The wife filed for divorce soon after, and he still thanks me to this day for saving him from an even bigger financial disaster. Telling someone they are going to get divorced is not easy; it can always be misunderstood or misinterpreted. But I really felt the urge to be the messenger, so I did stick my neck out. As a medium I genuinely feel an obligation to pass on the message I receive, at the cost of being misunderstood, so I am not left with feelings of guilt or regret.

DREAMS INFLUENCING LIFE PATHS

St. Francis of Assisi was born into a very wealthy, prosperous family of a silk merchant. As a young lad, growing up in an elite environment, he indulged in fine music, poetry, lavish clothing, and other luxuries and was known to spend generously. Sometime in his early adulthood, he started to observe his dreams closely and see profound meanings and guidance presented in them, which gradually caused a change in his mindset. He was no longer interested in pursuing a carefree life that failed to fulfill his soul. The dreams he had were clearly pointing to another path, one of renunciation and poverty. Many of the themes he noticed in his dreams were those of leadership, such as ones in which he was prominently leading a group of people on a spiritual path. The message was clear to him, that he needed to break away from his present life, and, renouncing his father, his wealth, and his home, he wandered into the streets, embracing his life as a penitent. He went on to establish the Franciscan Order, preaching the virtues of poverty and the worship of nature.

Sometimes dreams can portend a significant career- or life-transforming event by displaying something obscure or contrary that at first may seem incomprehensible. Like in the dream of St. Francis, dreams will repeatedly remind you that something that seems implausible at the current moment will indeed take shape in the future, however incredulous it may seem. This highlights the importance of recording your dreams and reviewing them periodically.

Visions, Ghosts, and Apparitions

WINSTON CHURCHILL

A vision can happen in so many ways, almost like a dream, while your eyes are open, not closed. There is a fascinating account of a vision described by Winston Churchill, the former prime minister of the UK. While he was deeply absorbed in the act of painting his father's portrait, he felt a sensation. Upon turning around, with his palette still in hand, he noticed an upright figure seated in a red leather armchair; it was his father, who had since passed. His father looked vibrant and healthy and was engaged in preparing his cigarette holder as he was wont to do. Churchill recounts his reaction of having no fear, yet standing away, while having a prolonged conversation (this happens when you have a vision: you are aware that you cannot approach the person/animal, whoever it is you are having a vision of). After the long, delightful conversation, Churchill's father vanished suddenly just as he had appeared.

The first vision, like that of Winston Churchill, that I had was while driving at night in the middle of a thunderstorm. There was a heavy downpour, and I could not see a thing. This was in the days before the internet, GPS, or cell phones, the days of the oversized physical maps, which I used extensively since I spent a great deal of time in the car traveling long distances. The memory of that night is deeply ingrained in my memory, although it has been decades since the event. On my way home that night, from an official conference that was in a town 100 miles or so away, my only thought was to get home safe and snuggle up with a warm blanket. The weather was miserable; it was pouring cats and dogs, the visibility was poor, the highway signs were blurred, and I kept my eyes peeled for fear of missing my exit and prolonging my trip. Although I was calm and relaxed, attentive, and alert, I inadvertently took an exit in somewhat of a trance state, which overpowered me. I veered off onto a country road, which was unrecognizable, pitch black without highway lights, with no car in sight. As I drove on, I heard a voice tell me that I was okay, and I would be taken care of. Still driving, I happened to glance to my right, and the scene totally entranced me. I pulled over and observed the most bizarre sight I had ever seen. In the background was an old barn, which looked incredibly ancient, with little windows. Out of the small front door, a young girl emerged with an old-fashioned wooden pail, the kind I have seen only in fairy tales. This young girl was dressed in garb that was probably two or three hundred years old; her skin was like peaches and cream, her eyes a glistening blue, and her gaze compelling. She looked directly at me while I still sat in the car, and some sort of energy transpired between us. I heard a voice tell me that this girl was me in another lifetime. As soon as that statement registered, I broke out of my trancelike state with the stark realization that I was lost in the middle of nowhere on a dark, deserted country road, in the pouring rain, with no clue to find my way back. Again, I heard a voice direct me to take the next left, where I would then see the sign for the highway. Fortunately, following the direction, I found my way back in no time and reached home safely.

This extraordinary experience explained so much and clarified the situation and circumstances I was going through at the time. This revelation provided many answers to questions I had, and I was able to apply the information, find closure, and move on. More importantly, this event opened and expanded my mind to accepting experiences of a somewhat paranormal nature, and to bravely face them without any fear. Regarding this experience, I have often been asked if I had seen ghosts or phantoms. My explanation to this question is that a soul that has passed can sometimes appear as a ghost or apparition, but not a building. If I could clearly see a barn, with windows and doors, that couldn't possibly be a ghost. The whole sequence that appeared before me was like a movie set, complete with action. It was not restricted to just one sole action; in fact, it was so orchestrated that I was led to the area, made to witness the scene, then safely guided back to my destination. There is no doubt in my mind that I was "shown" the answer that I was seeking. For some reason, I have observed that driving long distances alone can be a very meditative experience, inducing a trancelike state or facilitating a connection with divine sources.

Often, when one is going through deep grief, sadness, or depression, even extreme disappointment tinged with regret or loneliness, one tends to connect with the cosmos, which then sends you a signal or message of comfort to relieve you of your painful emotions and soothe your angst. A delightful visitation I once had was when I heard of my sister's wedding to be celebrated. Unable to travel such a long distance to attend it, I was filled with despondence at not being able to be with her on such a momentous occasion. One day, deep in thought as I returned from my daily walk, at the foot of the driveway my little dachshund called Sheeba, who had passed many years ago, appeared right in front of me, wagging her tail. She almost seemed to console me as if to say, "It's okay." My beloved pet, resplendent in her brown, shiny coat, which appeared almost like a halo in the sunlight, brought me so much joy and consolation that the moment was magnificent. I was overjoyed, momentarily abandoning my thoughts of regret and disappointment, to luxuriate in the vision before me, which filled the void in my heart. They say there is nothing like the present, and at that moment that rang true to its most exponential degree. I felt exhilarated, consoled, happy, and joyous, and this experience was the most delightful visitation I could ask for. One thing I have observed when I have these visions is that a strange awareness comes over me, some sort of ethereal knowledge that I cannot go near or approach the person/animal. Seemingly real, these figures are just to be witnessed, not touched.

Sometimes, a vision of a past life can be triggered while you are absorbed in some mechanical, monotonous activity. As I write this, I had an experience on Christmas morning 2020. I entered my studio that morning to do my workout, when I was unpleasantly surprised at the sight of water that was flowing toward me. The basement was flooded after a snow/rainstorm. As I was engaged in sweeping the water away toward the sump pump, the continuous action triggered a vision of a past life in which I was on a ship at sea. There was a powerful rainstorm, and I was grabbing at the sails, desperately trying to save the ship from sinking. At that moment, I could feel the water hitting my face and hear the cries of the crew on the ship. I broke out of this vision and brought my consciousness back to the present moment. Yet another observation I have experienced is that any activity with water has an otherworldly connection, whether it is a long shower, a soak in the tub, floating in a swimming pool, or similar experiences. Water has an undeniable power to stoke the active imagination. My best inspirations arrive during a routine shower, and I know they are coming from a higher source.

Then there are accounts of people in older homes experiencing poltergeist-like phenomena. Things such as light switches being turned on or off randomly or the television set being turned on automatically, weird noises at night, sounds of wailing, and so on. There are "ghost chasers" who are engaged for the specific task of chasing ghosts away. Ghost-hunting television shows have gained popularity in recent years. In old towns and countries where buildings and castles are centuries old, ghost tours and visits are much sought after by tourists. Paranormal sightings are measured by scientific equipment called EVP, or electronic voice phenomena. I have been on a few of these tours but have not witnessed anything ghostlike, which leads me to believe that ghosts may not like crowds!

I did however have an experience of seeing what I prefer to call apparitions. Several years ago, when I moved into a new home, changing locations by 100 miles, I witnessed a spectacular phenomenon. The town I had relocated to was new to me; the home was large, with a driveway that measured a quarter mile. The actual dwelling was set high up on a hill on a secluded lot of 4 acres. This was a drastic change from the previous home, which was set in a residential area surrounding other homes. This kind of isolation made me a little uneasy about the safety and security of the home. A few days after I settled in, on my way home from work, I stopped to pick up the mail. The mailbox was on the main street just before the driveway that led to the entrance of the home. As I walked back to my car, with the mail in hand, I happened to notice two women, one older and one younger. They stood firmly as if waiting for the bus or something (although there was no bus service at the time). They were of the ages of mother and daughter, and they looked at me directly, locking eyes with me as if they were communicating silently. They were dressed in clothes of a bygone era, perhaps the seventeenth or eighteenth century, and their complexion was very pale, but they had rosy cheeks. This kind of silent communication lasted but a few minutes, and then they disappeared as I stood transfixed by my car. What transpired during those few minutes was one of the most profound moments of my life, as they seemed to telepathically communicate to me that this new home was going to be safe and protected and that I had nothing to fear. My first impression upon seeing them was that they were neighbors who perhaps liked to dress in period costumes. I mean, this was a new town I still had to explore. At the time, I had just come out of a major surgery, moved my home and job to a new town, and was still working through the emotions of grief and loss, and this vision put me at ease and gave me the peace and comfort I so needed with adjusting to such major changes happening in my life all at once.

Upon introspection of this event, I gathered that these apparitions could have been my relatives from a past life, they could have been residents of a neighboring house in the past, or they could have been my spirit guides. I felt no fear whatsoever upon seeing them. On the contrary, I felt a sense of peace and joy, like what I felt during my near-death experience. Over the years, I have met my spirit guides, who do not include those two individuals. Having lived in that home for fourteen years, I can attest to the fact that their message was indeed validated. Even though the home was somewhat isolated, I felt safe and protected all through my stay. There were no untoward events or circumstances that were dangerous or harmful. My conclusion was that they were my relatives from a prior incarnation.

However, not all apparitions are those of the deceased. Living beings can also be perceived as apparitions, as in the case of someone who is close to death appearing before a relative to say goodbye. These types of crisis situations can involve either the person going through the crisis or the person at the other end, the percipient. Although, apparitions do not necessarily appear in a situation of crisis alone. In certain cases, visitations can also be omnipresent, one individual appearing at the same time in many physical locations. In the book *Autobiography of a Yogi*, in several instances Paramahansa Yogananda recounts events of the omniscience of both Babaji and Lahari Mahasya (Yogananda 2015). This is also termed bilocation, and there are several accounts throughout history of many cases in which an individual has appeared in more than one location simultaneously. The bilocation experiences of saints and mystics around the world have been detailed in many accounts.

7

Decode Your Dreams

ALEXANDER THE GREAT

In the fourth century BCE, there was a young child by the name of Alexander who was the son of the ruler of Macedon. His mother used to whisper in his ear that he was destined for a spectacular rise in the world, as the descendant of Achilles. This young man was presented with a copy of the Iliad by none other than the famous Greek philosopher Aristotle, who was his teacher. Perhaps this was the inspiration that ignited his vision to conquer the world. At night, Alexander slept with his copy of the Iliad under his pillow, taking this inspiration along with him wherever he went. Alexander went on to conquer Egypt, Persia, and many countries in Asia and the rest of the world, which earned him the title of "Alexander the Great."

Alexander's mother also whispered in his ear matters of his birth. She was known to sleep with snakes, and she whispered to her son that he was the son of Zeus. When Alexander was crowned pharaoh in 332 BCE by the Egyptian priests, he was coronated as the "son of the gods." Here is a classic example of a subliminal, subconscious manifestation come true. Later in life, Alexander was curious to find out if he really was the son of Zeus as his mother claimed in her whisperings to him. He undertook a perilous journey through the harsh, arid desert of Siwah Oasis to seek out the Greek oracle at the shrine of Ammon. Many heroes from his boyhood tales had consulted this oracle, which additionally provided the necessary validation for Alexander. The Greek oracles were reputed to communicate with the gods, and Alexander was excited to find out the verdict. Although he managed to successfully overcome the hardships of the journey, it is believed that the knowledge he gained from his consultation with the oracle went with him to his grave.

The very first step in decoding your dreams is to record them. In our modern times, technology has made it possible to do this in numerous ways. If you cannot keep a pen and writing pad next to your bed, there are other methods to complete this important function. You can always record it first thing when you wake up in the morning. The sooner you download from your memory, the more the information that is recorded. With our busy lives and hectic activity, dream information can easily evaporate if not addressed. Second, write down every detail or whatever you can remember. It may seem inconsequential at first, but a dream always has a deep meaning. If the information you recall is very paltry, obscure, or senseless, it does not matter. By writing or recording it, you are creating a pattern of memory recall that enables you to remember and recall more. Writing regularly also improves articulation and enhances creativity and active imagination. As you record a dream, the act of recalling your memory can sometimes trigger something important, maybe some small detail that you missed initially. This little detail could turn out to be the crux of the solution. Writing your dreams regularly can also build a discipline and add to your strengths and writing skills.

Once you have penned down or recorded your dreams, read them over a few times. Then reflect on them and meditate on them. Sometimes, after you have written and reflected on a dream, you can home in on the central theme of the dream right away. In this case you need only to confirm the interpretation by following the rest of the methods of dream interpretation. Decoding your dreams is like playing a game of charades or Pictionary, only with your eyes closed, something like a night-time charade—a significant charade that reflects your mental, physical, and emotional state of being, apart from other activities. The art therefore lies in decoding these dreams by making associations with symbols. Once you have a few collections of your recorded dreams, it is vital to go back and read them every so often. This is one way to validate precognitive dreams and make a note of them. Sometimes an event that has already occurred can provide valuable clues to a recorded dream, enlightening you and creating an "Aha!" moment.

Additionally, when you reread your written dreams after a period, you may make more sense of it through time. Especially when you dream of personalities and actions that seem a little odd at first. Moreover, symbols are loaded with meaning; a small symbol can translate to a paragraph or two of interpretation. There is the basic meaning, the subliminal meaning, and a metaphorical meaning as well. Dreams are made up of metaphors, puns, rhymes, and other factors that need to be decoded and deciphered. This becomes more important when you hear a conversation in a dream, or a song that you may hear in fragments. Hearing sounds in a dream is rather unusual; sound also acts as a symbol in dreams. You can sometimes hear your own name in a dream being pronounced by your spirit guides or relatives from the other side.

At times, you may hear a message that may be intended for someone else. A song is an example of sound in a dream. When you hear a song in your dream, examine the title of the song and reflect on any word you remember. Pay attention to the title of the song even if it does not appear in the dream. For instance, in mediumship readings, the medium may utter some incomprehensible or obscure words and phrases to the client while communicating with the spirit. What she relays is what she perceives she hears from the discarnate soul, and sounds can be a little tricky to interpret. Strangely enough, the client reacts emotionally to this obscure word since it makes perfect sense to her. To illustrate a personal example, which has been mentioned before, in a dream that I had in the early morning hours, I heard the word "car," but it turned out to be a precognitive dream that manifested in a few days, in which the interpretation turned out to be "card" as in credit card, not "car." This is how puns come into play in dreams, and adjustments need to be made while interpreting a dream.

SYMBOLOGY

How often have you woken up from a dream and remarked on what a bizarre dream you had, or heard someone make the same observation? Quite often, I imagine. It is not uncommon to dream of riding on a bus or subway train that suddenly morphs into a tiger beside you in a deep forest, while you wonder what is going on. During the day, our actions are so rational, logical, and intelligent that it is confounding, to say the least, that our dreams sometimes make no sense whatsoever. Dreams are filled with so many symbols, symbols that change quickly almost like traffic lights. The word "symbol" is derived from the Greek word *symbolon*. Symbols in our dreams take the place of words, phrases, and so much more that we rely on with our conscious minds. Whether we like the outcomes that manifest during the day or not, we accept them as rational results and events. Similarly, if the language of symbols was familiar to us, our "bizarre" dreams would also make perfect sense. The subconscious mind knows how to communicate only via symbols to the conscious mind; this is the language of the subconscious mind.

Akin to learning a foreign language, symbology in dreams needs to be understood first to accurately interpret and make sense of what it represents. Every individual has his own personal "dictionary" of symbols that his conscious mind is familiar with. The key lies in recognizing what these symbols denote to you as an individual. Each of us is unique in the way we think, feel, like, and behave. No two individuals, not even twins, can have a 100 percent match rate regarding their thoughts, feelings, actions, and experiences. Your growth and development are based on your experiences in life, and these are constantly changing. Your best friend in childhood is seldom your best friend for life. Similarly, your food habits, lifestyle, and choices, even relationships are rarely constant and unchanging. All these changes are observed by the subconscious mind, which then communicates to the conscious mind, accordingly in dreams.

Individuals are unique beings, and the dreams they experience are also unlike those that others experience. To cite an example, with reference to the natal horoscope, the placement of Jupiter, for one individual, in a particular zodiac sign would signify something entirely different than the Jupiter placed in the same zodiac sign for another individual, since not all placements are identical. So many other factors such as aspects, conjunctions, oppositions, and degrees are involved that the interpretation would differ. Symbology in dreams operates in much the same way, on the basis of your own individual connection to it. As the adage goes, "One man's meat is another man's poison." To clarify, a cat in a dream can be a positive symbol for a cat lover with thirty-six cats (I do know someone with thirty-six cats). The same cat appearing in a dream of someone who had a traumatizing experience with a cat in childhood could possibly be a nightmare. Therefore, before you dash off to consult a generalized dictionary of symbols, whether online or otherwise, pause to think of what the symbols in your dream mean to you. Dreams are highly personal and individualized. Your subconscious mind has specifically tailor-made it for you. One size does not fit all. Having said that, I do have a list of some general symbols you can use to begin with. You can always replace the meaning as and when it changes to your specification. Before you know it, you may have a dictionary of your own!

Below is a list of some common symbols that show up in dream queries.

House: self
Attic: conscious mind
Tower: superconscious
Basement: subconscious or unconscious
Tunnel: passage to another dimension
Cave: transformation
Living room: common everyday happenings
Library: study, knowledge
Wall: blockage
Office: work at hand
Music: spiritual connection

Water: emotions or unconscious mind
Window: outlet
Mirror: your soul
Bathroom: purification
Floor: base, grounding
Car: personal self
Street: public self
Bedroom: private activities
Front door: entry
Telephone: communication
Computer: work, social world
Pregnancy: growth (not necessarily a baby)
Colors: an alert
Sky: idea or concept, openness

There are many other symbols that can vary in interpretation on the basis of faith, belief, religious conditioning, and cultural training. For instance, the cross seems to appear frequently in individuals of the Christian faith, like the swastika or the symbol of Om for those of the Hindu faith. A similar case can be made of religious figures and godheads. Animals in dreams are very personal and contextual. The Indigenous people had an intimate relationship with animals, respecting them as equals of themselves, as spirit helpers, as animal guides, and as having the power to dream, reincarnate, and access spiritual realms. Many ancients considered animals as their twin souls, companions, and protectors; they even believed that the animal totem has chosen them. They carefully observed the activities and movements of an animal they connected with, as a guide to their own lives. The wolf, the eagle, and other creatures are still highly revered even today among Native Americans. Feathers and skins of animals were worn for protection. The shamans of Siberia clothe themselves with fabrics of bird motifs and feathers. Animals can also represent totem symbols for the self. Some cultures are embedded in superstitious beliefs that regard different animals as representing positive or negative significations. Similarly, animal worship creates its own dynamic regarding its association as a dream symbol. Worship of the cow, snake, monkey, or wolf is considered as a good omen in the dreams of these worshipers, so also of the lizard, which is the medicine animal to Native American dreamers.

Symbols can be very vivid and colorful in dreams. Dreams are created by the divine nucleus of the psyche and are somewhat three-dimensional in their meaning. To grasp their meaning, it is necessary to view them in the context of the whole picture. Symbols can have a basic direct meaning and an underlying metaphorical meaning and can even appear as allegories or puns in a situation. Intuition and mythical knowledge are extremely helpful in guiding the dreamer in the right direction. Symbols weave a story; they describe people, events, emotions, places, and things. By working with your dreams regularly, you can slowly begin to understand each symbol and what it means to you, since symbols are often life parables. If a symbol in a dream is something unrecognizable, bizarre, unknown, or unheard, you need to extend yourself to find out what it means. Go beyond the normal threshold of thinking to uncover what that signifies.

Once you identify the symbols in your dream, the next step is to put them in a sequence. Just like the ancient Egyptian hieroglyphics, which were independent stand-alone images but were read in the manner that each arrangement presented itself. Similarly, while you are interpreting your dream, generally one symbol alone does not reveal much. You need to read the symbols as they appear, as a whole picture. A dream is like a theater production of your mind; you must pay attention to several aspects of the dream. While watching a play in a theater, you look at the orchestra and observe the lighting, the backdrops, the curtain, the main characters, and the background. A dream must be viewed in the same way to decipher the meaning. Every little aspect in your vision and hearing is of paramount importance. Some important detail may lie in some feature that may not be as prominent at first but is nevertheless important. The lighting is of vital importance in a dream. If there is a little light (or darkness) in a dream, it means that the dreamer is in the dark or has little knowledge regarding the matter in the dream. If the light is superbright or highly illuminated, it could be a superconscious dream.

The characters who appear in a dream all have got to be accounted for. Every individual in the dream is playing a significant role; you need to observe carefully what they are doing as well. The direction and placement of these individuals in relation to you also need to be noted. Who is to your left, to your right, behind you, and so on, or if it is you in the dream, driving a car, which direction are you traveling in? Remember, dreams lack rationality, so you can be driving your car on the roof of a bus or anything. In one of my dreams, the car I was driving was traveling backward, and the oncoming traffic was going forward in the same lane. I was literally not just going backward but traveling opposite to the mainstream. As a matter of fact, at the time of the dream I did indeed feel as if my career was not taking off compared to the progress I had made earlier.

If the direction of the car is moving forward, the opposite is true, where you feel you are moving ahead in life. Another aspect to consider in any type of vehicle, including your own personal car, is who is occupying the various seats in the car.

Who is the driver, the passenger, or the back-seat rider? Accordingly, the positions will give you an idea of your direction in life. If you are driving your own car, you may feel that you are fairly in control of some current aspect in your life. If you are in the passenger seat, you may not have total control of that situation. If you are in the back seat, it may be an indication that you need to exercise more control regarding the situation. Or that you are unable to have a say or do not know how to express yourself in that situation.

If you are riding public transportation, such as a bus, train, plane, or subway, you are concerned about a collaboration, an association with others such as a partnership or group, or some team event. How the actors in the dream behave is how the event in your life may play out. If you are silent in the dream while others may be taking a more active role, it can indicate that you need to speak up or make yourself heard in some event in your waking life. Conversely, if you are causing a disturbance of some sort in the dream, it could be a warning for you to take a more passive approach regarding the event. It all depends on the actions and reactions of all the passengers (actors).

Feelings and emotions during the actual dream experience can categorize a particular dream as good or bad. Some dreams can cause bodily energies to shift and create physical reactions such as goose bumps, sweats, and headaches. Nightmares can cause physical reactions such as screaming, sweating, and heart palpitations that may sometimes awaken you. When this happens, it becomes imperative to note down the dream, since it could be significant, signaling its importance. Laughter, mirth, and feelings of joy and ecstasy are also emotions that are significant pointers to the type of dream manifestation. A visitation dream brings great joy and happiness whether from a loved one or spirit guide. Therefore, noting down your feelings during and immediately after the dream experience can provide you with broad clues in the interpretation. There are instances when you wake up from a particularly disturbing dream and find your hand placed on a certain part of the body. Refer to the chakras to interpret the hand placement following such a dream experience. Some precognitive dreams have awakened me in this fashion, and upon observation I noticed my hand placed on the solar plexus area, which connects to gut feeling and claircognizance. Immediately, I am alerted to the significance of such a dream.

Another important aspect in decoding dreams is to notice the surroundings. If you are outdoors, it could indicate a matter concerning the public or someone other than the dreamer. Alternately, it could describe the dreamer in public, his outward behavior, or how he thinks the world perceives him. Sometimes you might be in a public place in a foreign or unknown country. Make a note of the comfort or discomfort felt in such a dream, for it could very well be a past life vision. If it is a past-life dream, you will see repetitions of the same theme. Homes are often highlighted in past-life dreams.

I had a dream in which I traveled to a foreign location. The palace I was seated in had elaborate furnishings that were of a different period. There were murals on the walls, and no electrical lights. I was conversing with someone, remarking on how I missed my pet peacock, when I heard the cry of a peacock. As I rose from my seat to go outdoors to see the peacock, suddenly a large cheetah appeared at my side, and I awoke from the dream. My analysis of the dream was that it was a visit to a past life. This past life was one in which I was a member of royalty that was killed in that life. In the dream, the cheetah was my animal totem that rescued me from an impending disaster. Following this dream experience, when I have other dreams of a castle or luxurious palace, I make a conscious attempt not to enter it. This seems rather uncanny, but it happens very naturally, not out of fear but out of a knowing. A knowing of avoiding the witnessing of a traumatic event.

Animals in dreams can thus be identified as spirit guides. You can also have more than one animal totem as a spirit guide. One effortless way to find out your animal guide is to examine your own interests and likes. In my case, I am besotted with the cheetah print. In my wardrobe, there are innumerable clothes and accessories, including shoes and some furnishings as well, with the cheetah motif. The dustpan, fabric heating pad, and several household items are also of cheetah print. Currently, I even have a face mask made of a cheetah print fabric. What you are attracted to is indicative of what is meaningful to you. If there is something you are drawn to repeatedly or excessively, that is a sure indication of its power in your life. I also happen to love faux snakeskin fabrics and materials. Passionately fond of snakeskin print, I even posed with a live snake for a photo shoot wearing a snakeskin print bathing suit. At the time of this event, my awareness of this subject was not so broad. Therefore, it was not a deliberate action on my part, but rather something that evolved organically. The knowledge that the deity of the ruling asterism of my ascendant in the natal chart also happens to be represented by a snake was something I learned many years later.

These are some of the events and circumstances that provide clues if you are open to receiving them. Presenting themselves in your daily life, animal totems remind you that they are around to be called upon when you need them while astral traveling or even during meditations. It is believed that there are guides both on the physical and astral plane who sometimes rescue you if you cross certain barriers of the astral plane that could be dangerous. The aforementioned dream has proved to me that the spirit guide can sometimes be an animal functioning in the same capacity as protector. Animals that we consider wild, dangerous, or harmful in our waking life are our allies and companions. They are available to offer help, healing, and protection. They act in the same way as spirit guides do, as guardians and protectors. The shamans and Native Americans refer to these guides as medicine animals. Just as we call upon our spirit guides to aid and lead the way, an animal totem can also function in an analogous manner in journeys and travels. You can avail of more than one animal at a time too.

DREAM OF HOME

If the dream takes place in your own home, it concerns a very personal, private matter of the individual. Home represents privacy and individuality. In a vast majority of dreams, a home does not appear exactly as it is in waking life. In fact, you just have a knowing that the strange building you see in the dream is your home. The experienced dreamer, however, can see the exact home in the dream. This could also be a clue that it might be a precognitive dream. A dream taking place in your own home is an intimate matter about your own self. Only in the privacy of our homes do we take those filters and masks off. Likewise, in the dream of a home, there is no mask or disguise. What you see is what you get.

THE MEANING OF COLORS IN DREAMS

As in life, so in dreams color plays a vital role. If you dream in color like me, consider yourself truly fortunate, since not everybody does. Some people dream in black and white. Color can be a symbol by itself; an additional meaning can be had by the object or other thing as it appears in the dream. Colors are present everywhere in the world around us, in the blue sky, the green leaves, and the multicolor flowers. Present in the clothing we wear, the food we eat, the surroundings in our homes and offices, color is that important addition we cannot do without; it is an indispensable part of our lives. Life in just black and white is rather unthinkable. Our health and well-being, our moods and emotions, and our hobbies and psychology all are defined by color. We often use expressions of color in our speech and communication, by saying such things as "I am feeling blue" or "I am in the pink of health." The color spectrum, with its various hues and shades, contains a wide range of meanings depending on its brilliance and luminosity. Dreams with brilliant color can highlight an important aspect and underline its context. Astral dreams are characterized by their magnificent colors, and the vivid hues are so spectacular that they seem otherworldly. Each color and its shade denote something specific. As mentioned before, the meaning of a particular color provided here may not resonate with you; this is just a general guideline.

BLACK

The color black is generally regarded as something dark and depressive even in dreams, signifying loneliness, sadness, and other negative emotions. Again, the personal association and color preference need to be considered before jumping to a conclusion. Black is a popular color in general, used for clothing, décor, cars, and other utilities. Since we are surrounded by so much black in our daily lives, the way that black appears in a dream is rather important. Depending on the context of the dream, black can play a key role in the interpretation. Generally black has a negative meaning of darkness, hidden secrets, loneliness, mystery, and even sadness, since it is worn in mourning. Black can denote formality, as in a tuxedo suit, secrecy, and aloofness. As the darkest color in the spectrum, black can also stand for rebellion and disgrace, as in "blackened" or "blacklisted."

BLUE

Blue is a positive color denoting the sky, water, and truth, as in "true blue." It can represent emotions, feelings, thought, harmony, peace, and relaxation, as in ocean or spa settings. If the object in the dream is a crystal such as sodalite in blue, it refers to a connection with your spirit guide, representing a kind of introduction. Dark blue on the other hand, can lend itself to a shade of black in its nature, as in "I'm feeling blue."

BROWN

Brown represents the earth or Gaia, and a lighter shade of brown can signify earthiness, friendliness, and a sense of being grounded or stable. Instilling a need to seek more solid goals or seek material security, brown is a modest, down-to-earth, conservative, reserved color, seeking quiet and privacy. A darker shade of brown, as in slush, can mean murkiness, lack of clarity, even obstacles.

GREEN

Green is a fabulous color in dreams, representing life, health and healing, growth, nurturing, and fertility. Symbolizing nature, beauty, and the environment, green is also the color of the planet Mercury, which stands for communications and media, as well as the color of money. A darker shade of green that merges with black or brown can have a negative implication of envy, jealousy, and revenge, as in "I'm turning green with envy."

RED

Red is a color with multiple meanings. Here it is imperative to judge the inference in the entire context of the dream. The intensity of the color is important. Red is the color of romance, passion, and all that Cupid stands for. Red represents the root chakra, seeking material desires. As a color that represents the planet Mars, it could also signify anger, temper, danger, violence, and war. In many dreams, red appears as a sign for blood, indicating a needed health checkup or a warning, as in "red flag."

ORANGE

Orange is a fun, playful color that symbolizes friendliness and a bright outlook in life. Representing the rays of the sun, orange is a bold, vibrant color that is welcoming and open, enthusiastic, adventurous, even innocent and childlike. Orange in a dream can speak of the need to become more lighthearted and playful, getting in touch with the child in you.

WHITE

White lends itself to purity, innocence, cleanliness, and tranquility. In the West, it is worn by brides, in the East by widows. White can also represent angelic images, a feeling of openness or readiness for new opportunities. A white dove is a symbol of peace. White can signify the need for a new beginning, starting from scratch, or a blank canvas.

YELLOW

Yellow is the color of the sun, and the solar plexus is represented by yellow. A bright shade of yellow denotes feelings of positivity, brightness, happiness, and joy. A murky shade of yellow is less positive, the color of jaundice, fear, and sickness.

GRAY

Gray can literally mean a gray area, an indefinite concept or idea, dull (as in "gray sky"), confusion, hesitation, lack of courage, or a lackluster outlook. This may indicate a desire to remain neutral, detached, or inactive. Being more of an observer than a participant, not wanting to be in the limelight, and aloofness are other meanings.

PINK

Pink is a variation of red, usually denoting bright prospects, love, affection, and friendship. Discarnate spirits generally show up in dreams and visitations with pink objects such as flowers, balloons, or ribbons as a sign of undying love, comfort, and protection.

PURPLE

Purple, representing the higher chakras, stands for higher consciousness, spirituality, devotion, divinity, heightened intuition, and psychic ability. Also, as a symbol of royalty, purple can indicate some higher energy materially. A darker shade of purple can indicate a strong drive, sexual energy, and passion.

GOLD, SILVER, COPPER

Gold, silver, and copper colors appear rarely in dreams, and the object, the action, or the context of the color is the determining factor. In general, they represent enhancement and growth. For instance, in one of my dreams I saw myself as the Statue of Liberty, raising a gold wand up as high as I could. Shortly thereafter the price of gold skyrocketed. A little interpretation exercise here: the Statue of Liberty appears in a shade of green like the color of verdigris, representing, in this case, money or finance. The gold wand in my hand is representative of the metal gold. This is the way you combine all the symbols in the dream and link them to derive the meaning. You are probably wondering if I bought some gold after this dream, and yes, I did.

As with every other detail in journaling dreams, pay attention to the color, the shade, the object, and your personal preferences, as well as personality traits, in determining the meaning. If a color repeats itself in recurring dreams, that is a sure sign that some aspect of it will occur in waking life. As we grow and mature, we also change. Our preferences, hobbies, likes or dislikes, and circumstances also change, which could reflect the meaning of the dream accordingly.

NUMBERS IN DREAMS

Numbers play a vital role in our lives and our dreams. Time is made up of numbers, essentially, and we are constantly talking about TIME, which is numbers in motion. We say things like "racing against the clock," "no time," or "time will tell," referring to the concept of numbers in the bigger, macrocosmic picture. Each number is important for its own meaning, sequence, or vibration. A number can represent an archetype of the unconscious; it can be a symbol by itself carrying great meaning and potential. Whether a number appears alone as a single entity in a dream, or whether it appears in a sequence or group to indicate other meanings, numbers can indicate a variety of scenarios. A number can signify a date, a month, a year, an event, a birthday or significant day, an address, an age or a period, or an era. Personally, we all have lucky numbers, dates, and days that we hold sacred whether we are playing the lottery or planning important events in our life. These "lucky" numbers are significators, archetypes that follow us in our destiny and life choices. We may pick a particular number at the toll booth or gas station or grocery line, on the basis of our proclivity toward a certain number. Numbers in dreams give us clues or pointers that are translated from waking events to dreams, to remind us that it is "TIME." This could mean that it is time to vacate, enter or exit, or count down to a significant event in life. Numbers in dreams are the subliminal calendar of life.

Pythagoras, also known as the father of modern numerology, put great emphasis on numbers and their influence on our lives. He felt that the universe held the key to the science of numbers, and in the nature of the sacred musical harmony and geometric shapes. In his system, all double-digit numbers were reduced to a single digit except 11, 22, and 33, which were considered as master numbers and therefore indivisible. Each number has its own frequency and vibration as it appears in dreams. Sometimes dreams remind us that it is "time" to execute something or face some event. A specific number or sequence of numbers is drawing your attention to participate in the choreography of the event. Each number vibrates with an individual personality just like colors or symbols in a dream. When numbers repeat themselves in dreams, it reminds you that a certain important event may take place in the future.

Sometimes numbers can appear in dreams as a quantity of objects, such as three birds or three people in the same setting, three trees in a scene, or three balls. They can appear in pairs or patterns, in groups, or in diagrams or designs, as a place or denomination indicating price or quantity.

Number 0 is essentially empty, nothing, just a circle. In dreams, however, the 0 can represent a whole complete circle that is within itself, all encompassing. A 0 in a dream can also represent a mandala, the beginning of something more—in this case, potential. I had a dream in which concentric circles were evolving in and out of one another in the manner of a kaleidoscope, which meant several events occurring from a very obscure point, changing shapes, directions, and colors. The number 0 can be thus interpreted as well.

Number 1 usually represents the start or beginning of something new, such as the first day of school or a new job or event, and therefore represents the monad. This number can also represent the self, individuality, and ego, reminding you to pay more attention to yourself. A strong and creative number, the number 1 represents ambition. Alternately the number 1 can represent the lonely self, not having the support of others or having to go it alone, facing the necessity to make challenging decisions. On the other hand, it can also be overly dominant and egoistic, as in "I am number 1."

Number 2, being even, could indicate a pair of something, balancing, or equaling something; it could also indicate a partnership or intimate relationship and mutual understanding. As a negotiator, the number 2 can be patient, thoughtful, gentle, sensitive, and supportive. Sometimes it could mean facing a dilemma, or that a difficult choice must be made, or having more than one option, which can be stressful. Being overly sensitive, timid, easily hurt, or locked into passivity can be other associations of the number 2. Number 2 also represents the moon, which is exalted in the second zodiacal sign of Taurus.

Number 3 is an open, friendly number indicating art, creativity, and imagination. Like orange, the number 3 is extremely outgoing, positive, communicative, and optimistic. Uniqueness, imagination, out-of-the-box thinking, and a youthful approach to life are some of the characteristics of the number 3. However, this can also denote excessive artistic tendencies and creativity that can cause a scattered, unfocused mind with no concrete plan to follow.

Number 4 is balanced, grounded, earthy, and complete. The number 4 represents a square, which stands for conservative, demanding work; cautious, extreme practicality; and lofty goals. This is a dependable and consistent number, but it can be too fixated and inflexible and not amenable to the opinions of others. In dreams, this number can give you clues regarding the four directions (north, south, east, and west) or represent a structure such as a home or office. Representing builders, number 4s have great discipline and stamina to achieve their goals.

Number 5 is harmonious, bold, social, versatile, adjustable, adventurous, and restless. Symbolizing the planet Mercury, the number 5 is just as quick and mercurial, and impulsive. The number 5 can easily blend into any environment or situation. This number is overly flexible, spontaneous, and bored easily, seeking new opportunities and adventures with an incredible appetite for change. This number can also be too loose to conform to any one idea or concept, which can lend itself to versatility on the flip side.

Number 6 is the caregiver, loving and sacrificing for a cause. Cooperation, partnership, friendship, collaboration, generosity, group activity, loyalty, warmth, and harmony are other attributes of this number. A very Venusian number symbolized by the planet Venus, this number can be service oriented, loyal, and generous to a fault. This number can also indicate being nostalgic, revisiting old memories, looking back, and invoking love, affection, joy, and ecstasy.

Number 7 is a deeper mystical number seeking enlightenment and spiritual growth. Representing the planet Uranus, the number 7 is a seeker, researcher, and investigator who probes, scans, and analyzes all the mysteries of life. Being a wise, intelligent number, the seven is not satisfied with artificial information or fluff. Rather, the seven likes to withdraw to ponder the meaning of life, in an esoteric fashion. This number can indicate an introvert, a loner, or a recluse, which might be somewhat limiting. In a dream the number 7 could imply a week, seven days or months, or even seven years as an indicator of time.

Number 8 is a symbol of mastery symbolizing the planet Saturn. Another conservative number that is doubly more solid than the number 4, this number seeks perfection and sets up a high standard to follow. Denoting success, wealth, prosperity, and growth, a cycle of infinity and eternity, the number 8 is highly organized, neat, and tidy. The eight is about gratitude, about acknowledging blessings, and therefore represents both the material and spiritual worlds.

Possessing a tremendous amount of confidence and personal achievement, the number 8 can be inflexible and somewhat rigid, overly materialistic, and less philanthropic.

Number 9 is a highly spiritual number denoting rebirth and transformation. This number represents humanitarian deeds and actions and a selfless and philosophic attitude and points to a path of personal evolution that may be ahead. Representing the planet Mars, the number 9 has great courage and bravery. Growth, higher learning, devotion, and dedication can be attained, since the number 9 is the last single digit before 0 and therefore can also mean the end before a new beginning. This is a highly tolerant number that is sympathetic and nonjudgmental. Being a highly occult number, the number 9 can point to a lack of materialism and practicality. The number 9 can be reminiscent of the end of an era or period, the end of a chapter before you proceed to the next phase. Being too sacrificing and empathetic is one of the negative aspects of the number 9. The spirit number 666 when added and reduced also comes to 9.

Number 10 is primarily number 1 and 0 combined, giving the number 1 more power and strength. It indicates enormous confidence, ambition, abundance, wealth, great satisfaction, completion, and fullness. This number is highly elevated, as in the case of a pioneer, inventor, creator, and entrepreneur.

Number 11 is the first master number of intuition, spirituality, and partnership since it adds up to number 2. Being a higher vibration of the number 1, this number connects us with our inner wisdom. As a cumulative of the number 2, the number 11 can have some common traits of the number 2.

Number 22 is the master builder, like the number 4. This number highlights new consciousness, growth, and insight. Like the number 2, this is about balance, equality for a higher good, precision, and learning.

Number 33 is the master teacher, placing love above all else, a good educator and communicator, serving others to uplift and elevate them. This is a powerful number of exaltations. Sharing some vibrations of the number 6, this number can be sacrificing.

Numbers in dreams can appear as pure numbers, can repeat themselves, and should be interpreted in the entire context. If numbers repeat themselves, pay attention to all meanings of that number and dissect it to extract the advice.

8

Visitations and Spirit Guides

Jung himself describes the significance of his spirit guide visiting him in his dreams, whom he referred to as Philemon:

> *I observed clearly that it was he (Philemon) who spoke, not I. He said I treated thoughts as though I generated them myself, but in his view, thoughts were like animals in the forest, or people in a room, or birds in the air, and added, "If you should see people in a room, you would not think that you had made those people, or that you were responsible for them. It was he who taught me psychic objectivity, the reality of the psyche. . . ." He confronted me in an objective manner, and I understood that there is something in me which can say things that I do not know and do not intend.*

—Carl Jung, *Memories, Dreams, Reflections,* 1989

This revelation of Jung speaks of his belief in the afterlife, spirits, and visitations as entities from the other side. Jung clearly credits Philemon with developing his skills of objectivity and psychic nature. If you believe in reincarnation or life after death, the prospect of experiencing a visitation from a departed soul would be increased. Many Eastern societies are raised with these beliefs, which makes it easier for people from these societies to communicate very naturally with their loved ones. Mediums and shamans from ancient times have communicated with dead ancestors to receive advice and information. This is not a new phenomenon, although it has been gaining popularity of late with the gradual transition of medical doctors from skeptics to believers. Carl Sagan, the well-known astronomer, describes his own experience with visitation thus in *Parade* magazine:

Probably a dozen times since their deaths I have heard my mother or father, in an ordinary, conversational tone of voice, call my name. They had called my name often during my life with them. I still miss them so much that it does not seem strange to me that my brain occasionally will retrieve a kind of lucid recollection of their voices.

This sort of experience happens more often than is recognized and reported. In fact, sensing spirits is not just restricted to vision but extends also to emotions, smell, and taste.

As Madame Blavatsky points out, love has no limitations of time and space. Our loved ones from the other side are anxious to connect and communicate with us. We need to turn on our receptive channel by being open to receiving loving, comforting messages from them. In addition, some of the messages may also contain important clues that provide solutions to an ongoing dilemma in our lives. For instance, messages that can provide practical answers such as the location of the missing will, choosing the appropriate college or university, or even advice on investments. I have often received messages from my father about the financial markets, sometimes warning me to be more prudent and avoid risky investments, which proved to be highly beneficial, just as he would have advised me in his lifetime. The veil is thin between the incarnate and discarnate souls. There are times when we are more psychically tuned in, and our abilities are heightened to receiving communication from the spirit world. Practicing the techniques mentioned in chapter 3, "Dream Your Reality," can sharpen your skills and heighten your vibrations to connect with loved ones and spirit guides.

Visitations from departed souls in dreams are more lucid than other dreams. You will remember them the next morning, in detail. Since they are usually very brief, the message is on point and memorable. Feelings of euphoria, joy, and happiness abound when a departed loved soul appears in a dream, and these feelings can extend into the next day or days. Grief, loss, depression, extreme anxiety, and other negative states of mind can sometimes trigger a visitation from a parent. These beings show up in dreams to console you, to encourage and support you, and to lift you up from your depressed state just as they did during their lifetime. Sometimes in a dream you get the feeling that your parent is sitting on the edge of your bed, or lying beside you, which feels like a physical connection. Sometimes the sensations also extend to the sense of smell. When my great uncle visits me from the other side, I can smell his brand of tobacco. This type of ability to smell, called clairgustience, can also happen during waking hours when one is in a deep trance state. The throat chakra, if well developed, can aid you in the process of hearing and smelling in a dream. The throat chakra in its active, alert state can enable spirit guide or visitation experiences with sound, almost like the surround sound of a movie on the big screen.

Just a week after my dad passed, in a dream that I had, my dad visited my home in the United States. He was wearing his white outfit that he usually lounged in, and looked quite lost, and I was aware that he was not living. The amazing thing was that my house looked exactly as it is in real life; not a thing was different: the color of the walls, the couch, the foyer, the living room with its oversize windows, and the placement of the furniture—I could have had my eyes open; it was all the same. My dad sat in my spot on the couch, while I was in the library, in front of the computer. I was still seated when my dad got up, walked through the foyer, opened the front door, and ventured outside by the garage. Once again, even the exterior was an exact match to the real thing. My car was parked outside; he looked at it, then back to the street. He did this a couple of times, with a very puzzled expression; in fact, he looked a bit disoriented, as if to say, "Should I leave or not?" Then he came back inside.

This experience could not have been a lucid dream, because there was no sign of irregularity. Every detail in the dream was like I had my eyes open. After some reflection, this awareness dawned on me, that this was a visitation from my dad while he was still making the transition to the other side. He was quite bewildered that his presence went undetected in my family home in India, so he visited my home in the US, where my husband and I were present, hoping he could be recognized.

In another dream I had when I was first pregnant, young and naive about spiritual matters, my mother, who had just passed, appeared with a solution to my physical discomfort. One night, I was tossing and turning with a strange burning sensation in my chest. In a state of being half asleep and half awake, I sensed an image of my mother, who explained that it was heartburn I was experiencing. She then told me to walk over to the medicine cabinet in the bathroom, where I could find "Rolaids" on my husband s side of the cabinet. Now fully awake, I went over to the medicine cabinet, and there was the container of "Rolaids" just as she had described. Upon ingesting some of the Rolaids, I felt instant relief and went back to bed. I had never heard of or experienced heartburn before, and this medical lesson was, on one hand, truly educative and provided a timely cure.

Visitations can also occur by people on the physical plane. This is a sort of dream telepathy with a picture. One of my friends who is an actress has dreams in which a veteran male actor appears with advice on what projects to accept, and other career guidance. This kind of information is invaluable, whether the source is originating from living or departed souls. If it is a visitation from your spirit guide, it is possible that you have been ignoring him/her during waking hours, and his appearance in this fashion in your dreams calls your attention. Visitations can also occur in a waking state, in an altered state of consciousness, where you perceive someone standing before you, giving you instructions or guidance.

SPIRIT GUIDES

A Spirit and a Vision are not, as the modern philosophy supposes, a cloudy vapor, or a nothing: they are organized and minutely articulated beyond all that mortal and perishing nature can produce. He who does not imagine in stronger and better lineaments, and in stronger and better light than his perishing and mortal eye can see, does not imagine at all. The painter of this work asserts that all his imaginations appear to him infinitely more perfect and more minutely organized than anything seen by his mortal eye."
—William Blake, quoted in Arthur Symons, "Life of William Blake," in *The Complete Poetry & Prose of William Blake* (2008), 35

William Blake received extraordinary inspiration and ideas from spirits that he adapted to his art, which enabled him to cleverly create and produce the materials for his paintings during a time when the availability of art materials was scarce. In this manner, Blake applied the guidance he received from spirits directly to his waking life.

We all are assigned spirit guides when we start our journey on Earth. Whether we see them or not, they are constantly with us, guiding and protecting us along the way. There are many ways to establish your relationship and strengthen communication with these guides, who can be your ancestors and deceased relatives from any lifetime, ascended masters, or angels. If you are open, your spirit guides become more visible; they can also appear in dreams, meditations, and visions. Spirit guides are your SOS team, providing you with insight whenever you need it. As an artist, I have a spirit guide who was a master impressionist. Every now and then when I linger too long over completing a piece of art, he prods me to finish and sign off. Just like that. Other ways they communicate with you are through music, dance, and intuitive readings. Spirit guides also show up when it is time to leave the physical plane. They are present to accompany you and lead the way.

This is an interesting account that was revealed to me by a close friend. Her father came close to death twice before he died a few years later. On the prior two occasions, he was extremely critical, hospitalized, and barely conscious. The family, fearing the worst, started to prepare themselves for what might be the end. The father who was a very spiritual man, told his family that his spirit guide appeared to him and said that it was not yet his time. My friend's family was unsure of how to process this information. A few days later, the father was sent home in perfect health. This happened a second time a couple of years later. The father was taken ill and required immediate medical attention. Once again, the spirit guide appeared and told him it was yet again not his time. This time around, my friend's family was hard-pressed to take this seriously. Much to their surprise, their father recovered. The following year, the father was taken ill and hospitalized; sadly, this time there was no message he had for his family. He smiled peacefully and said his goodbyes to everyone. A week later he passed away.

Spirit guides can give you specific information of your own health and well-being. They can pinpoint areas of your body that need care and attention, locations where there may be disease and discomfort. You can receive guidance about diet, exercise, and even physical activities that may aid and assist you in leading a wholesome life and lead to better health. Spirit guides function as your partner in life, leading you toward the books you need to read, aiding you in spiritual growth, and boosting your confidence. One effective way of accessing your spirit guides is through dreams. Before you go to bed at night, make a request to meet your spirit guide. Be open to receiving, since your answer may arrive in many forms, as a definite person, an imaginary person, a feeling that is overpowering, or even a voice or a sound. For people with a strong clairaudient ability, the voice will be prominent; you may not see the face, but you will hear the voice. Once you have established a contact, be sure to record the details in your journal; you can then easily contact your spirit guide outside a dream, in a meditative state as well. Remember that they are always there with you, watching over you.

One important aspect of a spirit guide is that although they may be present in your life, they are not a 24/7 service plan. At times, you are responsible for making your own decisions and they will not interfere, nor can you expect them to live your life for you. They are there to HELP you, not act on your behalf. There can be more than one spirit guide; you can also have new spirit guides as you progress through life and develop new interests. When I started painting, a new spirit guide came into my life, whom I appreciate very much. I even have the feeling my work reflects his style a great deal, but that is another subject. The way you communicate with your spirit guide can take many forms. Sometimes it is telepathically, at times through a song or a random message that at first makes no sense. Synchronistic signs may be placed in your path to make a connection with your spirit guide. In a grocery store, you may encounter someone who might say something offhand that could trigger a memory. You may express statements like, "Oops, I forgot to turn off the oven. I'd better go home immediately." This happened to a friend of mine. She was shopping in a grocery store, to which she had rushed since she was missing some ingredients while baking a casserole. She had turned the oven on, started to assemble her ingredients to make the casserole, and realized she was missing something crucial. She got dressed and drove to the grocery store and was in the act of selecting her items, when an elderly lady approached her and asked for help in reading the fine print of a freezer item. Her eyes fell upon the words "oven temperature," and she realized with a shock that she had left the oven on more than two hours ago. She dashed home in time to save what could very well have been a major catastrophe! These are some of the ways that spirit guides can send messages when they are needed, to help you and rescue you. The key is to remain open and receptive.

ANIMA AND ANIMUS

Jung explores the concept of anima and animus in detail and explains that the spirit guides that appear in dreams are beyond the realms of the anima and the animus. The anima is the female part of the male psyche, and the animus the male part of the female psyche. Shaped mostly by the feminine, the anima is the personification of a man's unconscious. The primary function of the anima and animus in dreams is to illuminate some part of your hidden self. This may sound like the shadow self, but it is not always negative or dark. Jung says that the anima acts as a mediator or connection between the conscious and unconscious. They are independent of our conscious mind. For female energy, the animus is a valuable tool for reflection and self-awareness. Very often the anima and animus do highlight some talent or ability that is latent inside the person. By spotlighting a dormant talent, the individual becomes aware of what he is capable. The shadow self, on the other hand, is usually depicted as a dark or negative energy.

Dreams of celebrities, such as famous actors, politicians, and rock stars, represent the anima and animus in male and female energy. A common query I receive is regarding the interpretation of a celebrity appearance in a dream. Well, for one thing, you know of them, but they are not aware of your existence. They cannot see or hear you as you see and hear them on screen, or other media, so they cannot possibly be thinking of you. Your thoughts about them manifest their appearance in your dream. Some aspect of their personality provides the common link. Perhaps the trait you admire in them is something you hope to have or do have or might desire to emulate, which can then stimulate the creative process. An interesting fact is that we are also attracted to a partner who is in some way reflective of our anima or animus.

I had a fantastic dream one night. My husband and I went to a hobby store for him and not me for a change. An older gentleman was showing him some wooden shapes, then he showed me on a canvas how to paint a small bird by making points to mark the shape. The paint he used was not a traditional kind of paint but some other material, and I could clearly see the bird. Then my husband and I walked out of that store and through other stores, where there was a restaurant just below, and an older female waitress was entering a kitchen area with used plates in her hand. She stopped us and asked me if she could thank me. I said yes, and she said, "Thank you." I was so touched because she was the second person; earlier that day, an older man had thanked me too. Then suddenly we were in another store, and I was trying out a pendulum that appeared to be from another era. It was wrapped in brown paper and handed to me. I thought this was a strange large thing for a pendulum. When I unwrapped the brown paper, there were two parallel wood hangers, like lines, with a small column filled with turquoise-blue stones. I held one end of this hanger-like structure, and a candle-like flame arose from the center, pointing up. The same older man appeared and said, "Yes, that is how you balance it." It was a remarkable dream of guides who answered me in my lamentation of how my work sometimes is unappreciated. Spirit guides often appear as older people in dreams; clearly, they have no ego or vanity.

9

The Astral Plane

The best songs are the ones that come to you in the middle of the night, and you have to get up and write them down, so you can go back to sleep.

—John Lennon

A client had asked me why the singer Tori Amos claimed that her hit song "Hey Jupiter" was inspired by a visitation of John Lennon in a dream she had. Tori calls the song a lullaby, meaning that she was lulled into sleep by the song. Therein lies the explanation of how the song originated. Tori manifested her hit song by dreaming and channeling John Lennon to inspire her. She says that Freddie Mercury sang "Sugar" to her in the same fashion. Apparently, Tori has connected to these famous musicians for guidance and inspiration.

C. W. Leadbeater in his book *The Astral Plane* describes this plane of existence as "*Kamaloka,*" as mentioned in the ancient Sanskrit texts. He divides the astral plane into seven divisions and describes the inhabitants and their characteristics. He further divides these seven areas into seven subdivisions, describing all the different entities living on the astral plane. The astral plane is the closest to the physical earth, which makes visitations back and forth from these realms very conducive to receiving information, guidance, knowledge, and, yes, even entertainment. With regular practice and focus, you can easily access the astral plane at will. In fact, when the body is asleep, consciousness is on the astral plane. Leadbeater elucidates the heightened abilities of someone when traveling in the astral plane as having enhanced etheric vision, and capable of seeing animated particles in the air.

"Kamacarin" refers to beings who can transport themselves at will like travelers. The Buddhist term *arahat* refers to powers like those of the yogis who can fly at will.

The astral plane is a fascinating dimension that by many accounts exists not high up in the sky but remarkably close to the physical earth plane. It exists above us, below us, and around us, therefore not confining itself to any specific location. In *Autobiography of a Yogi*, Sri Yukteshwar says, "There are many astral planets teeming with astral beings. The inhabitants use astral planes, or masses of light, to travel from one planet to another, faster than electricity and radioactive energies. The astral world is infinitely beautiful, clean, pure, and orderly" (Yukteshwar 1946). Leadbeater says that the astral plane is more like an extension of the physical plane. He divides the astral plane into seven subdivisions corresponding to the seven states of physical matter: earth, water, air, fire, ether, gaseous materials, and fermionic condensate. He calls these inhabitants semi-intelligent creatures of the astral life.

The astral plane is also considered to be the intermediary plane where the dead rest until they proceed to heaven or until they are reincarnated back in the physical plane. The astral plane has no limitations. Everything is perceived phenomenally as vibrations of light. It can be the fountain of youth; if you desire to be young, you can be young for as long as you wish. Which is why departed souls in dreams appear much younger than when they left the physical plane. I never cease to be amused at seeing my parents in dreams looking like they did when I was a child. The command and power of thought is the driver in the astral plane, which is truly an unlimited realm. This plane can be accessed in fully awakened states as well as in dream states. Being next to our denser earthly plane, our earliest experiences can take place in the astral plane. The first few visits to the astral plane can be phantasmagoric, overwhelming, and incredible. Entering the astral realm, the soul has access to spiritual realms and becomes aware of its own divinity.

Leadbeater refers to the Akashic records as being a record in the astral plane, or he says, "Records of the astral light," which is a sort of photographic data representing all that has taken place. These records contain information about the past, such as memories and events that can be accessed through dreaming and meditation. Madame Blavatsky says that plain thinking produces a form that is animated. The astral world is heavily populated. Elementals on this plane are the natural inhabitants and can be manipulated by sound, color, and number to animate things on the physical plane, such as the act of producing a ring out of thin air, like Satya Sai Baba, an Indian guru known for his mystical powers and healing abilities, as well as walking on water, levitating (like Daniel Douglas Home, a famous Scottish medium who was reported to levitate to a variety of heights), or treading on hot coals. These forces are directed by higher beings. Number is related to geometric patterns, sound is related to sacred geometry, and color is related to vibration. There is continuity in the astral plane, where life is nearer to reality than on the physical plane.

NATURE SPIRITS

Nature spirits are formed of astral matter so they can occupy things such as rocks. Such spirits have been written about extensively in medieval literature, where they are referred to as gnomes, fairies, pixies, elves, and salamanders and can assume a human form at will. These spirits live close to the earth plane and are visible to the advanced psychic. They can manifest in all shapes and sizes with great rapidity on the basis of thought. These little creatures love to have fun, cause mischief, and play practical jokes. They have some traits in common with humans and can assume a make-believe human form at will. I had a bizarre experience on one occasion when out golfing. I happened to hit my ball just off the cart path, a little into the woods. First, I spotted my ball from where I was standing, made sure it was not rolling and lay still, and walked over to the ball, which had since disappeared. Normally, my rule for ball hunting is restricted to 5 feet from the cart path, not in the thick woods. But I was sure I had seen it on the spot, and I was befuddled as to where it could have gone. Making an exception to my general rule, I traveled just a bit farther into the woods, and a scrawny-looking man suddenly appeared with the missing ball in his hand, which I took. I had no idea where he sprung from, and before I could thank him, he disappeared into thin air! When I related this to my golf partner, she was sure I was on something hallucinatory, but I assure you I was not.

Also inhabiting the astral plane are demonic beings and negative entities, just like here on Earth. The novice astral traveler must be cognizant of the fact that both good and bad energies can be encountered in the astral plane; it is further suggested to have a trained guide lead you at first. For the adept, however, astral projection can be fun and amusing. As you practice astral travel and gain proficiency with it, a deeper understanding of the relationship between the physical body and mind is gained. When you feel the exhilaration of traveling without the cumbersome "physical body," you can even see the silver cord that attaches the etheric double to the physical body. This silver cord is like the umbilical cord of the embryo; always present wherever you travel astrally, it is separated only at the time of death, just as the umbilical cord is separated at the time of birth.

ASTRAL TRAVEL AND
ROBERT LOUIS STEVENSON

The past is all of one texture—whether feigned or suffered —whether acted out in three dimensions, or only witnessed in the small theatre of the brain, which we keep brightly lighted all night long, after the jets are down, and darkness and sleep reign undisturbed in the remainder of the body.

—R. L. Stevenson

The well-known author Robert Louis Stevenson was said to have experienced bizarre, outrageous, psychotic dreams and nightmares: astral experiences that provided fertile, imaginative material for his novel *Strange Case of Dr. Jekyll and Mr. Hyde*, which not only was radical in its time but was spectacularly produced and printed within a short period of ten weeks.

For two days I went about racking my brains for a plot of any sort; and on the second night I dreamed the scene at the window, and a scene afterward split in two, in which Hyde, pursued for some crime, took the powder and underwent the change in the presence of his pursuers.

R. L. Stevenson authored an astonishing array of novels, putting to use his nocturnal adventures. He references his dreams in many of his literary works.

MY BED IS A BOAT
My bed is like a little boat,
Nurse helps me in when I embark;
She girds me in my sailors coat
And starts me in the dark.

At night, I go on board and say
Goodnight to all my friends on shore;
I shut my eyes and sail away,
And see and hear no more.

And sometimes things to bed I take,
As prudent sailors have to do:
Perhaps a slice of wedding cake,

Perhaps a toy or two.
All night across the dark we steer;
But when the day returns at last.
Safe in my room beside the pier,
I find my vessel past."

—R. L. Stevenson, *A Child's Garden of Verses* (1984)

OUT-OF-BODY EXPERIENCE

Also known as OBE, an out of body experience is a projection outside your physical body. This refers to any distance traveled, be it to the ceiling of the room, a faraway destination, or a not-so-far-away destination, to the astral realm and so on. In a near-death experience (NDE), the body can sometimes travel to the ceiling and watch the physical body, as has been reported in several actual cases by several psychologists and parapsychologists. In an NDE the body can reach astral realms as well, as has been my experience. In various accounts there have been experiences reported of seeing "the bright light" or going through "a tunnel." OBEs can occur differently in a variety of situations. They can happen spontaneously as an NDE, during meditation, or during other physical conditions such as hypnosis, regression, accidents, major surgery, anesthesia, dehydration, or any kind of physical shock or trauma. In an OBE, the astral body enters higher realms, making a connection with our higher selves through the chakras. These OBEs can also be induced by specific skills and techniques that are practiced and developed. In addition, hallucinogenic substances such as LSD and peyote can induce OBEs. A lucid dream is yet another way to facilitate an OBE. Generally, OBE refers to every experience outside the physical body, including lucid dreaming, NDE, and astral travel. There are, however, slight differences between these events.

NEAR-DEATH EXPERIENCE

In *The Republic*, Plato relates the story of a brave soldier Er, who had been killed in battle. When his body was taken to the funeral pyre ten days later to be cremated, he came back to life and gave a detailed account of his experience on the other side. Er narrated how he met other departed souls who were then shown their life reviews in detail, but he was exempted and made to return to his physical body, although he had no memory of how he returned. In book X, Plato refers to sleep as death's sister. In the form of twenty-two dialogues, Plato discusses the higher planes of reality and death as the separation of the incorporeal part or soul from the physical body. At the time of death, he says, the soul is greeted by a guardian spirit who ferries him in a boat along with other departed souls. Separated by the physical body, the soul has the power to think more lucidly.

The Tibetan Book of the Dead describes detailed rituals and ceremonies for the departed soul, which were designed to serve the soul on his journey after life and to console the bereaved family of the departed soul. There is a parallel here between Tibetan and Hindu funeral practices. The Hindus believe that the departed soul should be given a sacred funeral according to auspicious events such as timing, ancient rites, and customs to ensure a safe passage to the afterlife. The Tibetans view dying as a special art that entails specific instructions for the various stages of death. Like a protective ritual, elaborate preparations are made invoking deities in homage, since they believe that the departed soul may be surprised and bewildered to find himself outside his body at first. Not realizing he is dead, he may still inhabit familiar surroundings. In this state, the soul can travel through space and solid surfaces, attempts to be recognized by his relatives, and is confused as to why they cannot recognize him. Refer to my dream in chapter 6, "Visions, Ghosts, and Apparitions," in which I had a similar experience with my father when he died.

The concept of NDE is not new, being widely recognized and accepted in Eastern cultures, although it has recently become more popular and credible in the West, with physicians attesting to this theory with their own experiences. Dr. Raymond Moody has been largely responsible for this phenomenon, with his extensive studies, research, and dedication through his various publications on this subject. He is credited with coining the term *near-death experience* and developing the psycho-manteum, a device that is built like a chamber that is dark and enclosed, blocking out any reflection. Mediums all over have further popularized this device to communicate with spirits. I have myself experienced the psychomanteum in mediumship gatherings and seances where many genuine personalities from the other side have appeared in spirit and provided valuable information. An NDE is different from an OBE in that the subject is clinically dead, whether for a few seconds, minutes, or days, as in the case of Plato's character Er. Temporarily the heart and respiratory functions stop, and sometimes even the brain ceases to function.

Although death and reincarnation have been acceptable themes of belief in the East since ancient times, it was Dr. Raymond Moody who introduced this concept to the West in his book *Life after Life,* in which he interviewed many patients, clients, colleagues, and friends about their near-death experiences. Dr. Moody has painstakingly sought to prove the experience of the continuation of life after death, despite severe opposition and criticism from the church, peers, and other members of society. Dr. Moody's work upholds the principles in ancient Vedic texts about the journey of the soul beyond the physical death via several actual examples of cases that he recorded.

Dr. Moody has detailed the cases of his patients and colleagues in his book *Life after Life,* in which he has documented that NDEs are real and not caused by hallucinations. Every NDE is unlike another, although some similarities prevail. Some people describe a tunnel or a bright light or a shoot; some, a bridge; and others, a galaxy. A life review is displayed for some where all events in their life are portrayed in a vivid, rapid manner, which they recognized as having experienced. Almost like a flashback, the entire life experiences are replayed, which prove to be transformational once they return to their physical bodies. In a recent issue of *Hypoallergic* magazine, mention was made of how science has now found evidence and is accepting this theory of how the brain produces images of memories just before death.

ASTRAL TRAVEL VS. LUCID DREAMING

Astral travel is also an OBE. The difference between lucid dreaming and astral travel is that lucid dreaming can occur only in the sleep state, while astral travel, also called astral projection, can occur also in the waking state. There are special techniques than can be employed to induce astral projection. Retaining your memory during an astral trip is rather difficult once you return to the physical body. Training and practice are essential to remember astral adventures. One principal factor to keep in mind is that while returning to the physical body, you must remember that you are outside the body and need to come back gradually, and not with a jerk, as we often tend to do. Just like with a dream, you need to write or record your experience as soon as possible or you might forget it. A synopsis of your experience would suffice for the moment; you can always fill in the missing details and information later. This process does take time to build but will bring successful results the more you work at it.

The pleasures experienced in the astral plane are far greater than those on the physical plane. We see objects and beings only partially as three-dimensional on the physical plane; our perception does not extend beyond that. With training, on the astral plane we can add a fourth dimension to our perception by combining the physical and astral vision. This ability enables the astral body to travel through walls and other surfaces without any hindrance. Clairvoyant vision and esoteric development will enhance astral travel experiences, as would accessing the Akashic records, which requires a great amount of specialized training to read them with a degree of accuracy. Generally, people born with psychic ability use their etheric body often, as I do. In fact, this is how I have traveled to visit my father, who lived in India, some 10,000 miles away. Since it was time-consuming, expensive, inconvenient, and sometimes impossible to physically travel, I used to travel in my etheric body to his home, check in on him, and then, feeling satisfied, would return to my body. This was a marvelous way to see him and feel the peace of having done so. Since I was so successful in making these essential trips, I continued practicing astral travel even for fun. I started visiting friends in distant locations, places to eat, shop, and ethereally enjoy many activities. An astral traveler in the waking state has been referred to as a *sky walker* by the Native Americans. This could also include levitation, as has been performed by Indian mystics and Christian saints and others, which requires a tremendous amount of force.

In an astral visit I had in the year 2015, I made the intention beforehand that I would visit my mother on the other side. On my astral journey, I traveled through what seemed like five astral realms and then felt myself soaring higher to the other realms, where in a circle were seated all the Devas (divine beings or angels) along with my mother. They welcomed me as I joined them in conversation, and they assigned me a duty, which was to go fetch a little baby boy and place him next to a female relative of mine. He was a tiny, thin creature, not like his older brother, with one large tooth showing, which was rather odd for a newborn infant. In 2018, this young relative of mine gave birth to a baby boy. The funny thing is, he didn't have a tooth like I witnessed in my dream. This was quite bewildering only from a dream perspective, since I did not know what to make of it. When the child turned three, he broke out of his normally silent personality and started talking "nineteen to the dozen," which explains the tooth that appeared in the dream (meaning "toothy" or talkative). More information on the Devas and the Devic plane can be obtained from the books by Leadbeater listed in the bibliography.

LUCID DREAMING

Lucid dreams are not just vivid, colorful, and pleasant; they are different from regular dreams. These dreams occur when you are dreaming but realize in a somewhat awakened state that you are dreaming. Lucid dreaming occurs when you are in a full dream state and aware that you are dreaming, a type of metacognition. Generally, this occurs between the REM stage of sleep and the waking stage. This can even happen when you awaken and go back to sleep. At times, in this manner, you can reenter the previous dream to change and direct the outcome. There are several techniques to evoke lucid dreaming. Once you gain practice and experience, you can program your own adventures and films to enjoy. At times, lucid dreams can be triggered automatically, and in some dreams, where you are being chased or pursued, you can take control through your conscious mind and direct the outcome. If you wish to evade the pursuers, you can fly and land on top of a tree or you can end the dream by becoming awake. You can even create weapons to combat wild animals or other dangerous beings and have a blast doing so.

Lucid dreams can be like exciting adventures of the Jurassic Park kind. You can control these types of dreams since some part of your consciousness is alert. Exciting, fun, and adventurous, lucid dreams can take you anywhere: over treetops, high in the sky, and to the most unimaginable places. You can be any superhero of your choice. The ability to control and direct the action of lucid dreams contributes to the excitement and fun. This is a fantastic way to travel far and wide, anywhere you desire. Dr. Stephen Laberge, a psychophysiologist, has become the pioneer of research on lucid dreaming in modern times, with his extensive work on the subject.

There are many methods to check and validate a lucid dream. Dr. Laberge formulated the MILD (mnemonic induction of lucid dreaming) technique in 1980. His technique is based on a behavior called prospective memory, which is to make the intention that you remember that you are dreaming. The tips he suggests are to recall a recent dream as you fall asleep. Identify anything that appears strange in the dream, such as flying. Return to the dream and reiterate the intention to remember as if speaking to yourself and your subconscious mind. To keep the dream fresh in your mind, another tip would be to wake up in the middle of the dream. These tips strengthen your memory and the ability to recall your dreams.

Yet another type of lucid dreaming occurs when you are awake but dreaming. Called WILD (a wake-initiated lucid dream), it occurs in a waking state while you enter a dream. In my experience, this type of a dream is not uncommon but is harder to distinguish from mere daydreaming. Practicing the other techniques of lucid dreaming will aid in developing the wake-induced dream. Although some lucid dreams can be fun and exciting, they can sometimes be like nightmares, of being chased or attacked. In this case, you may want to exit from this dream by waking up. An expert lucid dreamer can take control of a precarious or dangerous situation and find a means to escape in the dream itself. For instance, if in the dream you are being attacked by vicious animals, you can direct yourself to fly above in the sky or climb a tree or even awaken from the dream. I often resort to this kind of escape in my own lucid dreams. Having a favorite tree or trees in waking life can be an asset while lucid dreaming. Like animals, a tree totem can come to your rescue in times of distress. For instance, when you are having a scary nightmare of being chased, in a lucid dream you can pick yourself up and alight upon your tree totem, landing on the branch or treetop and thus escaping from the perpetrators.

Even Sigmund Freud, the father of dream psychology, acknowledged the validity of lucid dreaming in his addendum to his popular book *The Interpretation of Dreams* (1900):

> *There are some people who are quite clearly awake during the night, that they are asleep and dreaming and who thus seem to possess the faculty of consciously directing their dreams. If for instance, a dreamer of this kind is dissatisfied with the turn taken by a dream, he can break it off without waking up and start it again in another direction—just as a popular dramatist may under pressure give his play a happy ending.*

Like the scriptwriter in a television series who must change direction and kill a character who abruptly breaks his acting contract and quits the show (in case you ever wondered why a character in an established show suddenly disappears).

Virtual reality has now become a tool to help people with overcoming PTSD and nightmares through lucid dreaming. Experiments are being conducted to find methods to induce lucid dreaming. Studies may prove that training with virtual reality, like playing games on a home video game console, could induce more flying dreams as well. Sounds like good news for people who like to play video games and are therefore more likely to experience lucid dreams. The therapeutic benefits derived from this technique can help prevent depression and anxiety and other nervous disorders caused by nightmares. A technique called imagery rehearsal therapy (IRT) is being used by therapists to cure people with chronic nightmares. This technique encourages patients suffering from nightmares to imagine dream scenarios with positive endings. Nightmares were experienced by large segments of the population during the COVID-19 pandemic.

REMOTE VIEWING

Remote viewing is one of the ways of projecting the body to a distant place to see something through the mind's eye, without the use of physical senses. Remote viewing was popular in the 1990s and was sponsored by the US government to determine military intelligence. In early esoteric accounts, remote viewing has been described as an OBE or a sort of traveling clairvoyance like astral travel. This is a highly controlled process that seeks definite results and can happen simultaneously in a waking state, or even in a dream or trancelike state. Ingo Swann, an American psychic and writer, is credited with coining the term *remote viewing*. Swann has further developed a system known as CRV (coordinate remote viewing), a psychic technique that enables one to transcend time and space and perceive people, places, or objects without physically being present at that location.

Conclusion

As you familiarize yourself with your dreams and make a connection with spirit guides and loved ones from the other side, there will be a definite shift in your outlook on life that will affect your relationships in a positive way. Being in tune with your energy aligns you with the energy of the universe, which will bring about peace, harmony, and bliss. You will notice synchronicities happening around you, further enhancing your potential for awareness and understanding your purpose on Earth to lead a more fulfilling life. By manifesting your dreams into reality, you will attain satisfaction, fulfillment, and confidence in your ability to create. Things you may have overlooked in the past will resonate with you, leading to self-knowledge and a higher perspective. Your unknown talents will blossom, and you will start to believe in yourself with a greater vision, which will help you lead a more authentic life. Discovering new skills and developing them can bring growth and foster new opportunities.

Information of a past life through dreams can help heal and provide clues to your karmic evolution. You come across important aspects of yourself that explain some enigmatic events that were hitherto a mystery. By releasing unnecessary fears and phobias, the path is cleared of obstacles that impede growth and enlightenment. Understanding the past provides clarity on understanding the present. Your goals and accomplishments for your current lifetime become clear and coherent. Intuition becomes your best guide, providing a boost in self-assurance. Listening to your inner voice, you find a determination to face fear and consternation.

By directing and engineering your practical life with your blueprint, new doors will open to growth and evolution. A successful manifestation of a dream into reality will propel you to new heights of glorious confidence and the power to achieve. Developing your intuition and understanding your dreams and how to interpret them could help you deal with situations in your life with more ease. Comforting yourself and others with the information learned through dreaming opens new vistas and alternative channels that were unknown. When you see evidence that you can create your own reality through the power of dreams, there will be no stopping you on your path to success.

BIBLIOGRAPHY

Barrett, Tracy, and Jennifer Roberts. *The Ancient Greek World*. Oxford: Oxford University Press, 2004.

Besant, Annie. *The Ancient Wisdom*. Adyar, India: Theosophical Publishing House, 1897.

Blavatsky, Helena. *The Secret Doctrine*. Adyar, India: Theosophical Publishing House, 1888.

Blavatsky, Helena. *The Theosophist* 31 (March 1910): 685.

Cheiro. *Language of the Hand*. New York: Prentice Hall, 1987.

Cline, Eric H., and Jill Rubalcaba. *The Ancient Egyptian World*. Oxford: Oxford University Press, 2005.

Subramaniam, Dr. K. *Astrology for Beginners*. Chennai, India: Krishman, 1984.

Coleman, Graham, Gyurme Dorje, Thupten Jinpa, Terton Lingap, and Padmasambhava Karma. *The Tibetan Book of the Dead*. New York: Penguin Books, 2005.

Cornford, F. M. *The Republic of Plato*. Oxford: Oxford University Press, 1941.

Dixon, Jeanne. *The Call to Glory*. New York: Morrow, 1972.

Finker, Carol. *Osman's Dream*. London: John Murray, 2005.

Green, Elmer. *Beyond Biofeedback*. New York: Knoll, 1989.

Hogue, John. *Nostradamus*. New York: HarperCollins, 2003.

Jacob, L. W. *Interpreting Your Dreams*. Coraopolis, PA: J. P. Pohl, 1988.

Jaffe, Aniella, Jacobi Jolande, Joseph. L. Henderson, Carl G. Jung, and M. L. Von Franz. *Man and His Symbols*. New York: Dell, 1964.

Jenkins, Cheiro Herbert. *Cheiro's Book of Numbers*. London: Herbert Jenkins, 1959.

Jung, Carl G. *The Archetypes and the Collective Unconscious*. Princeton, NJ: Princeton University Press, 1981.

Jung, Carl G. *The Interpretation of Dreams*. 2nd ed. New York: Macmillan, 1913.

Jung, Carl G. *Mandala Symbolism*. Princeton, NJ: Princeton University Press, 1973.

Jung, Carl G. *Memories, Dreams, Reflections*. New York: Vintage Books, 1989 (originally New York: Random House, 1961–1963).

Jung, Carl G. *Portable Jung*. New York: Viking Penguin, 1971.

Leadbeater, Charles W. *The Astral Plane*. Adyar, India: Theosophical Publishing House, 1918.

Leadbeater, Charles W. *The Chakras*. Adyar, India: Theosophical Publishing House, 1927

Leadbeater, Charles W. *The Inner Life*. Adyar, India: Theosophical Publishing House, 1978.

Moody, Raymond. *Life after Life*. New York: HarperCollins, 2015.

Nostradamus, Michel. *The Prophesies*. Edited by Alphonse Gottfried. Philadelphia: Gottfried and Fritz, 2015.

Small, Cathleen. *The Science of Mind Control and Telepathy*. New York: Cavendish Square, 2018.

Stevenson, R. L. "A Chapter on Dreams." In *Across the Plains*, 211–31. New York: Charles Scribner's Sons, 1892.

Subramaniam, K. *K. P. Krishman's Astrology for Beginners*. Vol. 5. Chennai, India: Krishman, 1986.

Symons, Arthur. "Life of William Blake." In *The Complete Poetry & Prose of William Blake*. Edited by David V. Erdman, 35. Berkeley: University of California Press, 2008.

Ullman, Montague, Stanley Krippner, and Alan Vaughan. *Dream Telepathy*. New York: Macmillan, 1973.

Wolman, Benjamin B. *Handbook of Dreams: Research, Theories and Applications*. New York: Van Nostrand Reinhold, 1979.

Yogananda, Paramahansa. *Autobiography of a Yogi*. Los Angeles: Self-Realization Fellowship, 1998.